www.patwiseseries.com

IN YOU

DON'T LOOSE IT

What will you rather settle for an Average life or a great one?

PATRICK WISDOM ODEY

CROWN THE CHAMPION

IN YOU

DON'T LOOSE IT

What will you rather settle for an Average life or a great one?

PATRICK WISDOM ODEY

Copyright © 2019 by Patrick Wisdom Odey

PATWISE SERIES

International copyright secured

All rights reserved

The author assumes full responsibility for the accuracy of the facts and quotation cited in this book.

If you would like to use material from this book, do well to obtain a written permission by contacting the publisher at bliss1_promo@yahoo.com. No part of this book should be reproduced by any means or shared on any platform without the permission of the publisher. Reproducing materials from this book in any form without the prior permission of the publisher will constitute an unlawful piracy and theft of the author's intellectual property.

Published by:

Blessed promotion prints

Area 7, Garki-Abuja, Nigeria

10 9 8 7 6 5 4 3 2

Printed in the Federal Republic of Nigeria.

First edition: February 2019

The publisher has provided access and a platform for speaking engagement.

Call +2348036213200,
ISBN: 979-860-237-318-9

Dedication

I would like to dedicate this book to my lovely parents, Mr Patrick Oblechor Odey & Mrs Christiana Odey who invested their lives in nurturing and training me to be a man of principles and God fearing. They are for me the crown of beauty.

In my journey of life so far, I met two precious families that have touched my life immensely in a good way, showering care and blessings on me. Mr/Mrs James & Favour Iwara, and Mr/Mrs Egbe & Obianuju Uwaifo.

To my late sisters Margret Odey and Mrs Christiana Sylvanus. My family members Friday, Mercy, Samson, Joel, Bridget and Joy. Thank you for your care, support and kind contributions to my life.

Contents

Acknowledgments … vii
Preface … viii
Prologue … 1
CHAPTER 1 … 10
THE GATE WAY OF EXCELLENCE
CHAPTER 2 … 20
BE A CHAMPION
CHAPTER 3 … 30
AWAKE
CHAPTER 4 … 42
WHO ARE YOU TO THINK BIG?
CHAPTER 5 … 54
WHAT IS ACCOMPLISHMENT FOR YOU?
CHAPTER 6 … 60
LAYING THE RIGHT FOUNDATION
CHAPTER 7 … 65
WINNING INSTINCT THAT MAKES A CHAMPION.
CHAPTER 8 … 70
AVOID THE WAYS OF THE FOOLISH
CHAPTER 9 … 75
THE LAZY MIND
CHAPTER 10 … 79
THE FOCUS OF A CHAMPION
CHAPTER 11 … 84
THE TRAP OF LIMITATIONS
CHAPTER 12 … 94
AVOID THE BLAME GAME
CHAPTER 13 … 100
BECOME AN ICON OF EXCELLENCE.
CHAPTER 14 … 105
THE BEAUTY OF A QUALITY RELATIONSHIP
CHAPTER 15 … 113
THE LAWS OF ABUNDANCE
REFERENCE NOTE … 118

Acknowledgments

I want to appreciate God for His tremendous kindness and love toward me. He is more than good to me. Coming in contact with men like Dr Paul Enenche and Dr Becky Enenche my spiritual Parents, Bishop David Oyedepo, Pastor Adeboye, Bishop Noel Jones, Bishop T. D. Jakes, Late Myles Munroe, Pastor Mathew Ashimolowo, Dr Bill Winston, Pastor Chris Oyakhilome, Apostle Johnson Suleman, and other great leaders that have poured the fire of faith in their souls into mine, coaching, teaching and grooming for excellence.

Men like Brain Tracy, Robert Kiyosaki, Donald Trump, Warren Buffett and Bill Gate that has influenced my mind in the business world to think big and work diligently to create a life of my own.

Men like Late Nelson Mandela, Senator Ben Bruce and other world leaders of our time that have inspired me greatly just watching them from a distance, a heart connection is forged. Thank you for leading an excellent path worthy of emulation.

The editorial insight of Mrs Felicia Oluwemimo Ozigi put into this work and her wealth of knowledge generously lavished on this project to make it a success. Your input is forever cherished.

Preface

Our live is a constant and countless push for self-discovery between the dreams we had and the ones we desire to make. There is only one proper response and it comes with a price, however, too much of guess work leaves many in wonder land without any clear advantage in life. The line between self-discovery and self-destruction is so thin than few will ever know. Bringing you to this line where you can separate truth from facts and learning through applications of precise information and guidelines will remarkably unravel the gem in you. You must of necessity set the pace for this Discovery and come out a champion with distinction and stars of honour.

Life cannot offer you anything new until you change the building block. Take clarity from here as your only way forward. It is a 360 degree polishing of a man or a woman you must be. A book never written in this form and layers before: Lean into it and see the person you become.

Prologue

When a gem is discovered it is ugly and dirty, but through the refinement processes its beauty, lustre, and worth grows in value. You are a growing beauty with possibilities yet to be tapped nonetheless; it requires a unique set of skills to polish out the gem in you from the bubbles of your life realities. The journey between self-discovery and self-attainment is desire. **Fortune is the crown of everyman – make yours by polishing the gem in you.** *Everybody wants to be fortunate but only few have come to see the fortune hidden within them.* Crowing the champion in you is life greatest decision you can make because people do not appreciate gems when it is in its raw state.

You must see and tap in to all the great qualities you possess to grow your worth. *If you cannot discover your inherent qualities and express them, greatness may elude you.* **(You must describe, define and deliver on it).** Greatness is an outcome of a life driven by focus and total pursuit of commitment to a course. **You are a crown forge it.** *The glory of a crown is shaped in its kiln and the beauty of every crown is in the value attached to it.* Therefore, **pay great attention to how your life is shaping out in the mist of your growth process.** Nothing increases value like attention to details.

COMMUNICATE YOUR VALUE

What is the true value of life? Everything in nature carries a unique life or gem in itself (created life designed as seeds) with a serving purpose for profit and value creation. To grasp the nature and worth of our lives, to appreciate the differences in people and to attract unique opportunity out of their situations, are all based principally on discovery, **admiration, perception** and **understanding.** Discovering the value of your life to you and others, produce the best out of an individual and reduce the risk of wasting one's life. Note: Your inner and outer qualities frame your value perception.

Individual value or worth can be added or subtracted, even redefined depending on the information you possess. ***A man with a proper sense of value for his life grows into a champion and a leader with generational impact.*** *Note:* A person's value can either be on a decline or increase per time. No middle ground at all. A life governed by the right *concept for living* wears the crown of power, good freedom and excellence as oppose to a life or people structured in wrong concepts. **The value of a man is drawn from the concept of his thinking. Until you see value in a thing, you stand the risk of destroying or loosing it.** *Nobody can increase the value of your life or allocate more to you, than how much you have judged your abilities, how much about your potentials and purpose; you have discovered and the qualities you develop and bestow on yourself.* You must know who you are and what you have to communicate your value. (Your value is born out of the unique difference you were made).

'The journey of significance begins when you identify who you truly are and tap into your uniqueness birthing life transforming solutions.'

A large population of the world today are going through a battle of life devaluation every day, consciously and unconsciously. Just with a little close look, you will discover how people have lost their sense of completeness, ability to dream and make it happen, with broken personality, trapped in a struggle, intimidated, oppressed and attached to thinking patterns that has covered their life beauty and glory. Many people are not awake to this consciousness yet or neither have they gain insight hitherto because it is easy to accept what is normal than to pursue an exceptional life.

People easily live by the views and definition of others for them because they hardly know little about themselves, within the *contest of their true value.* Do not depend solely on the value rating people have perceived or imposed on you because it is based on admiration or none and their understanding per time, which can change at any time. It is difficult for people to appreciate who you are as an individual abilities that rest within.) It is one thing to be misjudged by people, but it is hard on an individual who has lost touch with self on any plain of reality. Life struggles and altering decisions can make a mess out of men and women where constant failing experiences can almost become your identity. Nevertheless, *who you become rest on your value perception, creation and distribution.*

It is difficult for people to appreciate the greatness in you when nothing seems to appear great in an apparent situation, just on their own. In many homes today across the world, most parents cannot see anything deep about their children's worth, how much more an outsider. It is so because; people are outwardly connected than inwardly connected, they do not see your thoughts, the things you believe in, the things you are equipped to do and what you can become. It is a generational thing, a cultural disease and short-sightedness that possess the human mind. **People will rather talk you down than build you up.**

It is easy for people to lose sight of who they are in the face of being constantly talked down, oppressed by their own situation, consistently stripped of any inner beauty, boxed up and classified into a particular group, depreciated with careless words until they begin to believe that there is nothing really good about them, coupled with a sense of worthlessness that is engendered by oppression and all forms of human abuses.

Whenever, a man thinks less of himself and his abilities, he begins to dot behind every opportunity, venture less, cave-in, and act out of fear trapped in the image of his own mind. ***"Every man's life is agreeing or conforming to the image in his mind".*** No! Stop for a minute, **you are a master piece of God's grace and beauty.** Rejection from man does not make less of who you are; it only shows their inability to see beyond their little mind because in you are hidden a champion, greatness, a queen and a king. Belittling yourself is accepting that they have won or their assumption is right. **You are too special to look like somebody else – a copycat!**

You are a star per excellence and a smile to many generations. **Appreciation is a seed of love**, an image booster: especially when it comes from people close to you. Learn to appreciate yourself more than anybody else can do for you. It is those who have appreciated themselves enough that can see the good qualities in others. Respect people opinions about you when it matters, but do not consider it final mostly when they are wrong in their assessments. Many people today are buried in other people opinion about their life, living in the shadow, just expecting little out of life. *The truth is that you matter.*

Never judge a man based on the negative realities of his circumstances, but rather judge him based on the strength of his character. "*I drove taxi to finance my university education*" – **Mike Adenuga**. "*My teachers use to call me a failure*" – **Prime Minister Tony Blair**. "*I used to sleep on the floor in friends' rooms, returning coke bottles for food, money and getting weekly free meals at a local temple*" – **Steve Jobs**. "*I use to serve tea at a shop to support my football training*" – **Lionel Messi**. "*I didn't even complete my university education*" – **Bill Gates**. "*I was sexually abused at an early age 9*" – **Oprah Winfrey**. "*I was in prison for 27 years*" – **Nelson Mandela**. "*Whether you say YOU CAN or YOU CAN'T, you are right*". – **Henry Ford**. *You can be more if you choose to be more.*

Our deepest fear is not that we are inadequate; people see less of themselves than they are prepared to make more of themselves. Our deepest strength is in the fact that we are powerful beyond measure (to do whatever we set our mind on). *We ask ourselves, who am I to be brilliant, gorgeous, talented, and fabulous, actually who are you not to be?* We are born to make manifest the glory of God that is within us: *The Champion in you.* As we let our own light shine we unconsciously give other people permission to do the same.

The deepest desire in the heart of every man is to grow above his current position, current level of knowledge, weakness, environment, experience and living condition toward self-actualization. However, *you cannot make significant progress with your life living with the felling of inadequacy.* Every life lesson and experiences should prepare you for progress and growth. The danger is that our experiences can either make or reduce our capacity to grow and become all we should be. No matter your experience or condition, you were designed to make a difference. A deep sense of worth comes when people begin to make good progress with their lives and making quality impact on others.

Progress is the act of life. Those who make something out of their lives run on the strength of their own motivation. The desire for success or the fear of failure can become the trigger of motivation. ***Value yourself enough to attain greatness in anything you do.*** Moreover, without people making substantial progress in their work or pursuit after many attempts, they begin to gradually doubt whether or not they can make it. Face your doubts until you conquer it.

Have you ever wonder what makes life work for others why some just can't get ahead? A lot of factors are behind it. Please note: *"the race is not to the swift, nor the battle to the strong, neither yet bread to the wise, nor riches to men of understanding, nor favour to men of skills: but time and chance happeneth to them all."* (Ecclesiastics 9:11).

Everything is a picture of our value system: when a man knows the true value for his life, he spends his time well. ***"People lose or deploy time relatively to the amount of value for their life".*** Whatever value you attach to your life shapes the direct application of your time. *Life is measured by the decisions of your time and the amount of time invested into you or the lack of it.* Your training, influence figure and social environment shaped your sense of value, which contributed to the foundation for a successful beginning or a poor one. ***"The journey of a champion starts with the quality of his or her value system".*** Your value system creates your strength, passion, pursuit and accomplishment. ***The lack of value discovery, creation, distribution and pursuit produce average existence.***

Time is a burden without the fuel of a dream or the pursuit of passion. *Therefore, if you are too small to dream you are too small to succeed or win in life.* You possess within abilities beyond your current awareness to make dynamic progress, hidden unless you discover, value and apply them. *What you do with your time draw the line between a champion and a failure.* **All of life benefits are hidden in the decisions you make based on your value set.** Life does not punish you for what you lack, but for what you refuse to acquire and do. Dream now! Champions are known for their actions while non-champions are known for their inactions or for the lack of one.

All men have equal or different opportunity to succeed but not all take equal actions. Being a champion is not all about winning a title in a race or in a competition, it is you identifying your star or inherent ability and make the most out of life without regrets or recourse to any man; producing the highest form of excellence possible. Let nothing and nobody be your weakness. Let the idea of winning in life capture you in details, crown your own labour with the price of a champion. The top is for winners, therefore, think forward and you will move forward. Let yesterday's failure, setbacks, depression and all perceived obstacles become the fuel that drives you to the finish line.

THE RACE

The race of life is given, simply put, it is fixed. You can take it or leave it. You joined the race from the day you were born. Every man born into this earth is placed in the golden lane of opportunity. Whether you lose or win, you are a potential champion. **Every man is good at something equipped with a unique gift that makes him a winner in his own right. It costs nothing to be in the race, but it costs everything to win the race.** It is not how fast you run but what you accomplish at the finish line. *You can start something out of nothing where people expect the least from you. Give yourself a chance to succeed.*

THE SWIFT

In the race of life, you will meet men of different sizes, abilities, intimidating when you measure your strength against others. Develop your own pace per time and stay focus. **Speed without control is accident waiting to happen.** Know this, that fast does not mean victory all the time. Hence, don't run ahead of yourself into things that can eventually trap you. Grow according to your speed level with your eyes on the final prize.

THE BATTLE

Interesting as life is, it is not without battles. Some battles are cheap, while some are harder than you can negotiate for. In some instances, people become trapped in their battle cage in the box of fear, traumatised and paralyzed because of the intensity of the battle they face. *Never bow to the difficulties of life because battles don't last forever.* Grow through it and overcome it. All battles are winnable; discover your strength while you fight through your pain. ***It takes the combination of strength, wisdom, understanding, skills, provision, favour and profitable people to bring about victory in life.***

CHANCE AND TIME

Every day is an opportunity for success, victory and progress. If you must win in life take your chances seriously and maximise your time. Time can be invested doing the right things or wasted pursing the wrong activities without a set goal. If you don't know where you are going, people will offer you many directions. *Don't wait for people to give you a chance before you succeed.* Create one. Become resourceful and productive in all you do because, a diligent person attracts opportunities. Time is a tool of power if you appreciate it. ***Think result and profit before you engage time*** – those who waste time, waste their chances.

Make no mistake when you wake up every day, you write a page of your life with the golden pen of decision. If you were to write the last page of your life today, will you be satisfied with your current position? If you knew that you can take your life to a new height of accomplishment with the keys that will be delivered to you in this book, what will change in 24 hours? This book in your hands will be a catalyst to propel you into new horizon, once you think and accept the challenges it presents. I congratulate you for making this decision today. Remember that reading about the stories of men and women who are great achievers does not make you a success. The key to making your own story great is by projecting a wise shift. Hence, let your story be the next breaking news. *Call a friend right now and tell him or her about this book and help them get a copy after you have completed this action steps.* Pick a book or a diary and write in details what must change in the next six months and what you must do to effect the change. Create a perfect picture of all you should have and can become in five years in absolute details before reading further. Why is this important? It is because; *the life of hunting and gathering without a pre-design achieves little in the midst of plenty.*

Note: *A good plan with a focused execution can attack a poor history.* Develop an appetite for a giant stride; put your fear to flight and give yourself a chance to succeed. *Nothing can stop a man who hasn't stopped himself.* Therefore, push every button of faith you possess because it is time to break forth. Are you curious? Then trust me: **Curiosity is the engine for progress.** I bid you come, take advantage of the principles in this book as the pages unfold unprecedented light. Ponder through the introduction carefully before launching further and do well to call a friend, tell them you have it made. Introduce this book to a friend. To crown the champion in you out of this book, do well to pay attention and meditate on the principles embellished in it. Take it and apply for result generation.

CHAPTER 1

THE GATE WAY OF EXCELLENCE
Everything is a picture of our value systems

The equation for success, power and balance in life is in the instruction of wisdom. Lose it and endorse failure, value it and create success. Paying attention to details and secrets gives you the winning edge. What are you paying attention to now in your life? ***Are you creating value with your time or are you living the value that you are?*** It is up to you to discover it. Value conveys intention of purpose, direction of vision, appreciation, satisfaction, attraction and worth. Hence, make your life a power house of attraction and a continuous increase of value. *"The business of time is value".* Thus, pay attention. What value are you producing or marketing?

When your value chain rises in a network of demand, you will rise to extraordinary height but when your value drops, a fall is near. If you do not create a value system for living that will determine your rise, progress and stability in the long run you cannot measure your life worth. ***How you value the use of your time will determine the total output of your life.*** *Losing your time without a steady increase in value, payment, content, net worth and expansion is poverty looming.* Activity without equivalent value gained or added is waste. ***Average living stems from a poor value system.***

Know your disabilities and terminate them. Your time energy is only valuable when it diminishes your disadvantage and multiplies your advantages, your strength, and asset base, colour your relationship and significantly increase your power. (Including that of others) Weak value systems make weak men, while strong value system makes men strong. Only *attentive* people handle the business of life well and produce excellence out of everyday operation or actions, through a clear design and applied choice. If you must unlock your greatness, you must open the gate of excellence. ***"Value originators and distribution creates quality attention and promotes excellent***

lifestyle". *Good attention reduces the risk of failure and gives you the advantage of wisdom.*

The mind is the gateway to excellence: if you can't find and form value in it or with it, then it is worthless. Mind: *The element of a person that enables them to be aware of the world and their experiences, to think, and to feel; the faculty of consciousness and thought.* **"The worth of a mind is in the value it creates, the set of values he or she lives by and the value it sees in everything".** You make your value and your values make you. *A man must know his value and appreciate the difference in others to live his life well.*

People live by the values they seek. This is the master key to life and business. **The right set of value crowns a man with the mark of distinction.** People generally subscribe to the value they see in you, what they see in things or what you can produce. **It takes perception, learning, insight and understanding to create value in and out of a person.** (Your thinking shapes your value system). People performance and individual growth increases dramatically when they can order their priorities right and apply their mind to constructive use as value direct.

We all look at the mirror of value to see ourselves. **'Your world is as big as the values you produce or as big as the value that attract people and resources to you'** when people look at you, what do they see? ...It is content that creates attraction. *Your mind is a creative bank of power and wealth – open it.* You are too rich to be poor. **If you ever open the gate of excellence you will attract traffic of wealth.** Beauty is sustained where value is defined and where good thinking always produce excellence.

Without the force or features of value in a thing, there will be no demand or identification of worth. *Supply is an outcome for value demanded.* Demand creates supply, supplies produce volume, and volume accumulates power and power creates more value. It is our value system that generates ideas in us and the ideas you create informs your thinking and governs your life actions and outcomes.

People spend their lives where their value leads. The ultimate blueprint to greatness and escaping the average life is formed in the frames of our value systems. ***Results are the product of a man's value for time and the direction of his efforts.***

See a man on a downward fall; he has been living on a faulty system without any time for reflection and correction where necessary. ***Success or failure is hidden in the value system we adopt.*** Everything important is driven by the hands of *value givers*: it is the corner stone for human progress. They are value givers and value consumers everywhere. Value givers increase productivity, while value consumers split your energy bank. ***"Abuse is inevitable where value is lost".*** Where a man losses the value for his life, time, relationships and his work, he ends up abusing it and others as well by indulging in poor choices and destructive tendencies.

Value creates vision: until vision leads the way, you are heading nowhere. Until vision points at it, you cannot seize it, until vision sees it, you cannot conceive it, and until vision prepare you for it, you may wait too long. *Value is the capital for life transformation and appreciation.* Societies and individuals fail where the correct values are misplaced and misapplied. **Good value system arms the wise, while poor value system destroys potentials.** *Generate a supply value chain of wealth and you will gradually tap into the root of greatness.* ***A nation and her people are built on the value that defines it.***

Consistency of result is a proof of a vision led life. Therefore, you cannot build your life more than you are ready to accept the responsibilities of your vision. People manage more crises whether on an individual level or corporate level where good values don't govern their actions toward a lasting success. ***Vision driven by good value system makes you do only the right things, and doing it the right way all the time.*** Until you are looking for how to improve the quality and the quantity of your personal or organization output, you do not have a vision. ***Vision is the focus lens of your desired future.*** *"Vision is the preview of your life values"* vision creates your life calendar and patterns your productive energy into calculated activities. *"Your day is as good as the vision coordinating it"*. **It is the vision of today that makes tomorrow a future. What are the things you wrote down to do in six month? If it is clear to you make a picture.**

Value enhances possibilities: all you can be is in the vision steps you take. *A man is enslaved or freed by his value system.* Nothing changes fundamentally for any man or nation where their value systems remain the same. *What build a great life are the fundamentals of your values that create your ideals.* Everything you can be is on the scale of your value system. Everybody should be successful but only few end up with the crown of success. ***Everything rise and fall on our value systems because leaders see through the eyes of values.***

You must create a value system that can build you up for an excellent life by: 1. improving daily in vital areas of your life, 2. live with a sense of mission and urgency, 3. make yourself useful and approachable, 4. dwell on the positive things of life and build on them, 5. increase your self-esteem by solving economic, spiritual and social problems around you, 6. give no room for any bad character blemish that can possibly devalue you, 7. live a productive lifestyle, and 8. Never reduce your self-worth because of a temporal need for survival or become a tool of destruction. Become more by doing more for others and worth something on the table of appreciation. ***People do not crown mediocrity, only excellent performance.***

Value creates planning: the future of everything reside in a plan that under guides it because things do not just work out on their own, you work them out. **You are the director of your future.** If you do not plan it and enforce it, you exist with wishful thinking without a navigation focus. *Planning is creating results out of your time and meaning to your actions.* A plan should be big, rich and powerful enough to inspire and influence your drive daily. ***"Your life will always expand to fill the boundary of your focus per time".*** *Whatever you will acquire in life is waiting for a plan. (Think about it).*

A plan is your values on paper. The best way to spend your time is to bring your plans to fruition. ***A man without any value set makes no plans.*** It cost to live without a prosperous plan devoid of developing strategies. *Whatever you do not create in a calculated plan you cannot pursue effectively.* You can only develop an effective plan through the eyes of your value set. ***Destination, preparation*** and ***foresight*** make planning effective with measurable objectives or attainable goals backed by time specific actions completing a vision.

What is the best way to birth a plan? Define the focus of your vision and visualize your success destination with physical picture aid. Put a picture and a passion to it. Obsession is good as long as it is producing the right results. Know when to begin execution and know when to finish it because a finished plan is better than a delayed plan. *Timing is sensitivity to your hourly programs and budget or daily course of action.* If you do not set a time limit to it, you don't have a plan yet. Afterwards, become a wise and passionate risk taker. Never be afraid that your plans will fail. Doubt creates hesitation and hesitation prolongs success. Commit your plans to God and secure divine partnership; trust God to lead the way. Cost the total outcome of the vision with detail analysis.

Identify the available resources and the attractable resources that are lacking, and estimate or do a SWOT analysis that gives you full knowledge about your *strength, weakness, opportunities* and *threats* to develop a winning strategy. Know the demands and the daily task required to accomplish your vision, avoid all distraction until the successful completion of your plans. The key to profitability lies in your ability to match your resources, both *tangible and intangible* with your capabilities to seize the opportunities within your external environment to accomplish your set plans. Identify barriers that will limit your goals/objectives: be thorough, decide on direction that will be most effective, reveal possibilities and limitations for any strategic change. Do revise your plans to best navigate your path into profitable systems, individuals, communities, and organizations that can contribute to the fruition of your dream. ***Plans work if you work them.***

VALUE SYSTEMS THAT MAKES YOU A CHAMPION

a. *Know the value of your mind and Value your life* – until you know the value of your mind and how it governs your life, you will lack influence in the social order of time. **Give value to your life by building your intellectual capacity to deliver excellence.** Be relevant and a resourceful mind of influence in everything you do. Think global and give the best of the value you are. Make every small opportunity big by the touch of your input creating excellence. *Value creates value* therefore, be valuable - worthy of demand, compensation, appreciation and admiration.

b. *Value for time* – the value you have for time confirms the value for your life or anything else. *If your time expenditure is empty of a good future dream, steps toward your goal and result generating task, you are wasting life.* Your Value set makes time a valuable asset. All assets appreciate where there is control, focus of intention, investment of purpose, protection and multiplication of resources. Time well utilized equal future advantage however, the opposite is true. The balancing of time engagement equal the balancing of life. *"If you cannot track the value of your 24hours daily, you should not blame your failure or success on anybody".*

The value set that controls your time distribution affect the direct outcome of your destiny. *You do not manage time; you only manage your decisions and the outcome of your time investment.* What do you compare your decisions to daily? Always compare your decisions against its outcome. *'You are the picture of your value set'. Be wise.* You cannot set the direction of time in life because it moves with or without you. *You can only set your personal direction in time through effective planning regulating time or activities.* Nobody is richer in time or poorer in time. Always ask, is this the best use of my time?

c. ***Value for God*** – it is the first and the best step to nurture on the list and the most important. Never lose value for God's instruction and principles because it is in Him you will find your life greatest value. God created time and the elements that govern it therefore, ignoring the master and source of time is dancing with the chains and pains of ignorance. Being guided by the word of God crowns you in distinction here on earth and eternity. All producers have manuals guide.

d. ***Value for principles and governing laws*** - Know them and apply them correctly because ignorance is never an excuse. One of the laws of life states that: for every effect, there is a cause. You set the cause and you enjoy the effects. That is to say, you sow what you reap. Two, a man without a personal value for his life will lose it to anything. Third, only successful actions create success. Whereas, destructive actions create failures. Principles do not change with people, religion, climate, tradition, culture and colour. Ignoring principles and set laws reduce your chance of creating a lasting success. ***Laws govern time and influence all life outcomes.*** Those who break governing laws break down eventually. Laws gives you control over the outcomes of life.

e. ***Value the investment made into you*** – profitable existence begins with appreciating the capital investment made into you to make you a person of value. Most people abuse their privileges by letting time pass without any correct appropriation. You defraud yourself playing on your life investment without making the best out of it. If you do not value a solid parental cover, you abuse your provision. Do well to invest into your life and others.

f. ***Value your strength or your talent*** – no man is empty of substance, discover, develop and deploy maximally your potentials. Do not waste your talents because it will earn you your market value. Every talent is rich in substance to make quality and quantity appreciation over a life time when you polish it to fruition with precise information. You have it all in you to do your quantum leap, take your stage and make it big. Doubt is the only limiting factor trash it out. Do not let critics cripple your chance of succeeding. Allow people to make their input, but don't die under their label that puts you down than inspire you. *Watching your gift blossom into greatness is the best flash of success.*

    g. ***Value your connection or your relationships*** – to do more and achieve more, you must connect more with good people and relevant contacts. When you abuse your connection with bad character and insensitivity, you break the potential your relationship carries. *Succeeding with people is more important than succeeding alone.* People are life valuable asset that can support, promote, provide and connect you with opportunities. If you are married, family life is gold if you treasure it. Respect it and it will serve you.

    h. ***Value your seed*** – without the seed of action, there is no harvest of result. Until you plant your seed you cannot look for harvest. Sow into your dream, opportunities and wherever you expect result. Seed exist in different forms like ideas; money, efforts, time, thoughts, action steps etc. do not eat your seed during planting season. Protect your seed because the future depends on it. **Life is design with the beauty in your seed.**

i. *Create a lasting value system* – trade value for value. If your outgoing is greater than your income, stop and re-think now. You are a limited resources with little amount of energy to earn sufficient money for all your needs. Leverage your energy into life paying assets and systems through collaborative efforts more than your individual pursuit. *Once produced, forever working.* Produce fruits, solutions, innovate and offer a service that creates wealth for generations to come. *Live producing and die producing value.* Find the value chain that fits your set of skills, passion and training and fill that gap until you gain dominance. Never live by the salary or earnings you are paid to do a job. Do live by the wealth of the economic fruits you produce that can reach millions of potential consumers. Salary only pays bills, but a tree producing fruits will serve generations to come.

> *When the eyes of your understanding are enlightened through wisdom, you create values that are power craft for excellence and you generate steady progress for life. "Nobody can market you more than the value you express".*

CHAPTER 2

BE A CHAMPION

Life is a game of confrontation unless ignorant you stand a chance to win

The dynamics of everyday life is a process full of challenges, opportunities, griping feelings, night of silent tears in the cold hand of worries and the forging fire of hurting times, with strokes of learning curves as we look at the screen of change that can either make champions or victims out of the events of our lives. Man in the puzzle of confrontation relates with time by the choice that defines his hope, desires and expectation. ***Confrontation is the battle of desires.***

You cannot confront the day successfully without the battle field of desires. It is the current of our desires that makes us fighters. Becoming a champion means; Fight to win, fall but do not stay down, seize each opportunity as it comes and crush oppositions where and when you meet them. Preparation and self-development impacts significant knowledge for the fight ahead which is capable of crowning the champion you are. Every potential champion should live with the full knowledge of their contest, because of the things life throws at people daily, many have become less and less of their true personality or make-up and may never live out their packed potentials or mark time with their exceptional brilliancy. *Has life taking more from you than it has given to you?* (Left behind, deprived, forgotten, betrayed, robbed, oppressed and denied)

Note: never wait for life to give you anything before you maximise your time. ***Go for it as God direct.*** Considering the average life men and women live today under the struggle of economic changes and deprivation; poverty, wickedness, limited ideas, poor information flow, and the lack of access to capital, poor education, poor enabling environment and the confrontation from men and systems that tend to hold back rather than release forward. These are staggering realities one you must beat to fly. People have settled for a life of struggling and smallness today, because it is considered normal. *It is abnormal to* *settle for the life of struggle.* It is also abnormal to be lost in mediocre existence and trapped confuse about your life. Break that cycle today.

Growing in a world full of conflicts is a ball of difficulty to handle, as people lives revolve around fear rather than inspiration. The fear of the unknown, fear of failure, the fear of rejection, the fear to risk it, the fear of oppression, even death etc. fear produces torment, inaction, procrastination and makes men take half steps toward their dreams. **People who walk in the half or fraction of their abilities never measure up to greatness.** *Are you aware of what you have and how much you can do with it?* Hey… get the answer documented. An average existence breaks the power of individual expression of their potentials, expansion and limits human advancement in every aspect of life. **You cannot maximise greatness in the land of average thinkers mirroring their thought habits or with average thinking mind-set.** It takes courage to stand out and be counted where people see average survival as normal.

The environment often become dangerous for men who see average existence as a threat to their aspiration, and will have to live with clashes from opposite thinkers as they strive for excellence at all cost. Have you had people tell you, "you can't make it that far", "you are not good enough", "nobody in the family or in our community have made it that far" "and you talk big too much"? People most time unconsciously become road blocks and confrontational to other people dream when they have nothing to pursue of their own and where at most part they have failed. *Negative people come from negative history and the opposite is true.* Never leave your future to people approval rating as long as you are travelling the right path.

No two persons can live successfully together without the conflict of thoughts and desires. It is even difficult for a person to achieve total harmony of thoughts within themselves. There are conflicting thoughts within the walls of our mind that makes it difficult to have one single thought on focus. Nevertheless, ***"It is focused thinking and pursuit that births the champion in you".*** It is also a major fight between individuals seeking the same goal in front of an opportunity our own interest first. *Confrontation is the struggle for advantage, balance, control and the clash of power.* **Every mortal man lives for the pursuit of one significant power.** Therefore, life becomes a game of confrontations unless ignorant you stand a chance to win. "The conflict of our emotions is the biggest war of confrontation in any front of human reality". **Becoming a champion is accepting the challenge of a crown.**

No man can walk into the future without overcoming every day huddles of life. Knowing that you can succeed in your defined area of pursuit is a game changer. *There is no easy path to success; the only thing sure is that, it takes a fight to rise in life.* It cost to rise above mediocrity, but it cost more to lose critical fights that can change your life for good or for the better: mostly when all you have is a dream and determination. Nobody can live long enough without any resistance and possible opposition. If you must stand with the successful, you must take successful steps…be a champion. Every good vision that creates distinction or beats the norm or dares to break established structures, contrary to popular approval stand the threat of confrontation from people in the human society. The reason is simple, there are midst multitude of ideas; contrary conviction, receptivity complex, the diverse nature of man, individual stakes and group interest, and the wicked nature that influences the actions of men. **(People easily resist than they assist)**. What a free world, indeed?

To become a champion of your own class, you must break free from the traditional way of doing things; even if it means flouting the status quo once established. **Only traditional thinking stops people from living an exceptional life.** *Tradition conditions people into behaviour patterns that can either make or break them.* "Breaking free from your past into a glorious future is the journey of a champion". *Confrontation makes progress a test of character,* because only weak people die in poor customs. Every great civilization has withstood one form of confrontation and perhaps, every human progress has faced oppositions directly or indirectly. If you have not encountered any trouble, distress, unfair tackle, torment, and grappled with the hand of unfriendliness, then you are yet to rise to the place of (importance) in the arena of men's relative social order.

Please note; your life is an important piece of influence, because of the characteristics of your uniqueness, and because of the contribution you can make to the human race and its development. People do not always align with you because you have good ideas, powerful dream, blessed with extraordinary qualities, or cooperate with you when you begin to break new grounds in reformation, leadership and accomplishment. The negative forces of life are always in constant battle against the good forces of life, through human activities deliberately design to oppose at the end of the two spectrums depending on which side you stand.

The negative forces that inhabit the human mind create more destruction than it can sustain good in itself. (Like adverse hatred, bitterness, evil jealousy, wickedness and many more) men generally grow and flourish under a loving, protective, caring and nurturing hand which exemplifies the good forces in men. Nonetheless, *you cannot live without conflicts and crises crossing your destiny path.* Champions do not emerge in isolation and pretty waters; they evolve through life battles and common struggles known to all. But they are not afraid to stay alone if that is what is required.

Battles are significant because it forges strength in us to stand up for ourselves and be counted, or it can also reveal our worst fear and weaknesses. When the battles of life push you to the edge of despair, you need a voice command within your heart that consistently encourages you to stay in the fight. You need one voice of strong conviction, trust and power that helps to keep and protect your mind from fainting in the pool of stress. That voice of victory in you can either die thru fear or be developed to full capacity by courage to handle anything life throws at you until success emerges. ***"Listening to the right voice is the key to being a champion".***

Life victories are attained by the voice that guides our path. Even so, one negative voice in your mind can significantly affect the direction and your chance of succeeding. ***Our lives is built via the voice navigators in and around us because man is a listening creature*** *affected by sound energy. You are conditioned to fail or succeed by your voice programing.* We are surrounded with life threatening circumstances that are quite intimidating, screening and conditioning our abilities to rise over the daily confrontations and man-up to everyday challenges. There is a voice in every experience you encounter, it does not matter how loud it is because you can either go forward or backward listening to the voice of your heart.

Out of the cloud of your fears, setbacks and confrontations, you can engage the weak emotions inside and power it with all the resources available within your reach to win and conquer your fight. Life is in stages of growth, development, experience, understanding and establishment. Thus, do not let the process scare you. **Progress is a direct product of human initiatives and amour-propre or self-confidence.** The minute you begin to make substantial progress, opposition air their ugly head without invitation. (Nothing to be afraid of) Your will to live and conquer all intimidation is vital to becoming a champion in your respective area of pursuit or endeavour. Human intimidation doesn't go away suddenly, so why let it beat you? Fight back – resist until you conquer. *If you knew you are a conqueror, how will it impact your behaviour?* You take risk where others fear to try.

Never take any defeat final, mostly when it is related to your destiny course and your life purpose. *You cannot grow to your full capacity thinking like a victim of circumstance, belittling your strength, running from confrontations and succeed.* Successful people fall sometimes but they do not stay down. Quitting from a challenging fight does not make life less confrontational. *"Win your fight timely" champion's fight with winning strategy* running from a winnable fight only makes you lose total control of your life circumstances. **The pains of a loser are greater than the pain of a victor.** Think like a champion no matter the intense nature of your battle.

It takes an inspired mind to take down a motivated enemy. **Confrontation against your vision is an act of an enemy.** When a person become empowered or enthused against you by the wicked inspiration and power to draw from: mostly, when you become weary of the fight to be able to overpower his or her conspiracy. *Never take the history of an enemy lightly without caution and discretion.* Know your history well because 80% of your battles are rooted in your history (Both family and personal histories). Our greatest battle in life is men fighting themselves. **The enemy you won over yesterday or today have not given up on you.** Therefore, never make a quick assumption about any enemy.

Enjoy all victory carefully and respond to each threat strategically. Strategy with the right weapon positions you for victory timely. *Understudy your enemy and stay prepared always.* Draw inspiration from the pool of wisdom and make dynamic strategy for the season you are in because, a rigid man or an organization in a flexible and subtle war dies with a shot of ignorance. Be readily adaptable or responsive to new situations. **Precision makes the head of your enemies cheap.**

Every success you desire has its wing of confrontation. Prepare ahead of time to contain and eliminate them progressively. Become a man or woman of foresight with an ever ready action plan. You start failing or make little progress when your preparation is late. *Handle your threats before they arise: it is the wisdom for mastery. (Just ask the right question and findings).* **Life requires force to beat resistances;** the force of the mind, the force of action, the force of partnership, the force of divinity, the force to engage and eliminate. ***All enemies operate with subtlety, working in the shadow of your ignorance, building on your weaknesses and capitalizing on your quietness.*** Until you see your enemies clearly for who they are and gather the right fire force to rip them apart, you are just a victim in the midst of an unclear war.

Oppositions and confrontation exist with different level of power, structures of operation and capabilities. Their primary assignment is to stop you at all cost. **Enemies confront because they seek to conquer, disrupt progress, rule and dictate.** There are basically two types of enemies, the ones within and without. The enemies within have more destructive powers than the ones without. The proximity of an enemy is to study your weakness and produce access points for infiltration. ***When a man becomes his own enemy, he looses the crown of personal relevance.*** Develop the seventh sense of discernment to see and fish out enemies within, hiding in disguise as friends, staff and family relations.

Everybody have a devil trying to confront their progress, happiness, success and total wellbeing. You may not be able to stop an enemy to invade, penetrate, or gain certain access into your life, but never let them operate successfully when that breach is made. All enemies thrive on deception, lies, organize conspiracy, wickedness, and destruction, information gathering, binding spells and hiding under false image.

The blessing on a life attracts confrontation from the enemy. Men become bitter, hostile towards others with destructive behaviours not because they have done anything wrong against them. That a person is brilliant, very attractive, rich and wealthy attracts hatred, bitterness, strange attack and wicked conspiracy against them without any personal fault of their own. ***A heart empty of love is the devil factory for destruction.*** Protect yourself against the destructive tendencies of wicked forces around. Do well to commit your life to God completely because safety is of God. Watch closely against all enemies and equip yourself to handle all threats militating against your life, dream and purpose.

The overall purpose of an enemy is to make people labour in vain, give up on their dream, and make men experience demotion from their success height and see them suffering. If you take pleasure in seeing others suffer and fail in their pursuit without any cause, you are gradually becoming an agent of destruction. *If you have a dream, you automatically have an enemy because it is the light of your vision and success that makes you a shining star.* People do not suffer losses by accident; they are engineered by men and women with darkness in their soul. Pray that God will expose the enemy in the open interacting closely with your everyday life and the ones in the dark. Enemies can be physical or spiritual. The physical ones have physical powers, weapons, and operate through physical means majorly. A spiritual enemy embodies grave dangers because they have invisible powers at their disposal, weapons and operate through multiple platforms to perpetuate evil and treacherous acts. Note: spiritual battles are real whether you believe it or not.

What does it take to win against all enemies?
(13 strategic principles)

1. **Knowledge** – full knowledge delivers full result to the possessor of the light.
2. **Defence** – develop a fortified covering against all negative forces that is counterproductive. You can also run into a safety arm of trust to shield and protect.
3. **Attack** – be on the attacking position permanently and let your response against all enemies' action paralyse and exterminate their grip and possible trap over your life. This does not make a person violent but a proactive thinker not reacting after an action has passed down.
4. **Cripple their operation** – gain the right tools to stay alive and put your enemies down. Never be ignorant of the devices of the enemy. Enemies do not sleep; they live by devising wicked works day and night. Be alert in the spirit and the physical with deep sensitivity.
5. **Keep discretion** – let your actions never compromise your security and safety. Protect your head from cheap exposures and do not fall into the lure of the enemy. Reduce the risk of becoming a casualty.
6. **Work** – sleep when your enemies go to sleep, work when they are working. Sleeping when an enemy is working makes you a cheap prey.
7. **Gather intelligence** – gain spiritual Intel at the place of prayer before the all-knowing God. Develop a walk with God that

makes Him jealous of you. Use your resources to gather intelligence, see and discern motives quickly through a resourceful surveillance network. Men who whisper bad words against you in the secret are potential enemies waiting for the right opportunity.

8. **Avoid careless associations** – death falls on the head of the care free without caution or self-discipline. Associating with the wrong company is digging your grave without knowing.
9. **Pay attention to details** – schemers live in detail plotting. Little details from a vigilant observation minimize your risk of exposures.
10. **Use your head well** – out-think your enemies with quick and precise steps of advantage. Subject them to a permanent fall.
11. **Measure your opposition well** – never under estimate an enemy and never over-state your position of power. Do not assume you know your enemy well until you have totally conquered them. ***The enemy buried is the only one you knew. Enemies exist to be captured.*** Know your enemy monitory position over you, their strategy formation, communication network, execution patterns and equipment at their disposal.
12. **Be unpredictable** – never give an enemy the first advantage unless you have the last advantage in play. Keep them in a blind spot and study them quietly. If your enemies can predict you, then they can take you out systematically.
13. **Be equipped** – skills and training is your first advantage. Do not permit any weakness reduce your strength. The possession of the right weapon positions you in clear power to win. Be technically sound and indomitable.

Being a champion means an individual succeeding despite opposition, battles, death traps, and enemies conspiracy. Win your battles as there come. Be guided by wisdom, knowledge and understanding. No weapon is too small in the act of war. Therefore, gain one tactical weapon every day because wise and solid preparation leads to victory and success.

CHAPTER 3

AWAKE

Consciousness is the light of perception – find your advantage.

Professor William James of Harvard, "compared to what we ought to be, we are only half awake. We are making use of only a small part of our physical and mental resources. Stating the thing more broadly, the human individual thus lives far within his limits. He possesses powers of various sorts which he habitually fails to use."

Life is a growing perception of awareness. You will only become what you know and do. A large population of human in our day and age are lost in one way or the other in the valley of decision; looking, seeking help, pursuing, and searching for answers to life puzzling questions rocking the walls of their mind without any clear riposte. They are lost in the sea of muddled ideas, neglects, confusion, and uncertainty, blind to the future and the outcome of our choices. *It is not enough to have eyes but to use them to see well.* The eye of your mind (your consciousness) is your light of advantage in a world where men are for the most part lost and blind.

The journey of life and greatness begins when you can take mindful and sensible decisions based on understanding, of what is happening around **you** and **in you**; your inner state and your physical state: Becoming who you should be by a conscious act. Your destiny is connected to the events of your life whether good or bad, there give you clues and meaning in less revealing manners because the evolution of consciousness in us is stimulated through a gradual process, in seasons of human growth, trainings and in the strength of your awareness. Knowing how to respond to your desires, reason effectively, act and connect with the people and events that theatre in your destiny path and taking advantage of it is consciousness.

Nobody can build you more than your conscious ability to see, assimilate, gain insight, articulate facts, coordinate your actions, learn progressively, listen and apply strategic knowledge. To be fully aware of our consciousness means to consider in details. *Human consciousness has three core activities: feeling, thinking, and willing.* These three activities actually take place in our **soul**. We *form* our feelings, thoughts and acting in our soul and express them through our body. The more aware of this we are, the more conscious we are.

Many do not always know what is going on around them or in them to be able to do self-appraiser of their lives decisions, actions and direction. The evolution of consciousness in man helps him to become more aware of life unfolding truth and the underlying principles of time, through feelings, thinking and will as he engages his mind to respond to life demands and events through objective and rational thinking. *A man is loss when he cannot choose from right or wrong - consciousness; inability to differentiate, appreciate and follow wise patterns.* When considering human consciousness, it is not enough to say human beings are conscious and have consciousness. This state of being awake and aware differs from person to person and changes within each one of us throughout the day within the flow of emerging activities.

Perception is power. The way you think about or understand someone or something is power. Therefore, gain the right one. It will take the light of perception to see clearly the power in your decisions, perhaps you can avoid living in what used to be, and create what should be. *Only a conscious mind is aware of its possibilities and awake to its realities.* What you see in the state of vibrant consciousness is your first reality – it tunes us to the occurrence of our world and time. *Nothing is clear to you until you can appreciate or rejects it.* Only a man conscious of his need can respond to pain, invitation, fear and stimulating desires. *"Results flow out of the attitude of our mind".* Have you heard the saying, "you don't know what you have until you loose it?" it is so because people work, play, relate without being consciously awake on a deep level of recognition; because our **thoughts are passive not active**.

Weakness is an attitude of the mind, so is strength. *Capacity stems from perceived thought; consequently you are a building of your consciousness.* A man conscious of his personal weakness and the burden of his situation with the wrong conclusion think fear that is crippling in nature. **You can only exercise control in your life to the degree of your consciousness**. Whenever you can effectively control your thoughts, you have seen the light of perception. Knowing where you are and how to get to where you want to go, is the journey of consciousness. *'Life is wasted when a man is lost in his consciousness acting without self-control or applied thought towards a set goal.'*

IDENTITY CREATED BY PERCEPTION.

We live in a sensitive world where men and women are governed by the impression of their identity. People want to know how I fit-in in this life. *Who you see inside is what you express outside.* **Perception is self-identity crystalized.** It is how we see ourselves on a conscious level that we relate with our world. The impression on our senses gives us awareness, insight, some notion, estimation, belief about ourselves and total self-realization that forms our personality type. Identity search and self-definition can be thought-provoking for many. Identity crises is part of human struggles for relevance, acceptance and recognition as people try to portray certain image light or description, fraught to fit in, in to high-status groups, make and re-make themselves through pear pressure until they become a shadow of their real person. **It is easy to lose identity trying to be like another person when you don't have a clear picture of self.**

A person becomes unique and significant when he or she discovers their own unique individuality. The understanding of this complex reality cannot be based on popular opinions about you, but it must come from the ***discovery of purpose*** against popular opinion. *Sometimes, it takes a life time for people to really discover who they are or what makes them different.* Be awake. It is your discovered identity that builds your self-idea or self-image and your self-idea or image develops your self-concept, and your self-concept defines your inner and external abilities, and your abilities organise your world. **Your life revolves around your self-concept.** *Individual organization is a direct reflection of identity perceived.* (Your language, dress, choice, behaviour and your lifestyle) *"Your life is an echo of identity formed".*

We have become primarily part of a culture, experiences and traditions or societies where we carve our identities from our background rather than from our unique purpose or design. Identity shaped from your background most time is faulty perception because it is seen in the light of provision and privileges not purpose and endowed abilities. People generally form social identity through these life trajectories where they use it adapt to their collective world. *Extensive dependence upon others deny you the meaningful engagement of your life and deprives you of self-discovery;* where people develop cognitive blocks that prevent adoption of adult role-schemas in searching out their purpose, instead they engage in childish behaviour with an adult look *refusing* to see and reflect their identity.

They are those who *drift* through multiple thoughts and conceptions about themselves, never arriving at any conclusion dispirited toward the application of psychological resources *to see who they can be*, settling for anything convenient. They are those who are dissatisfied about their perceived image, due to high personal and social expectations or drive commit to a *search* dipper than surface existence to find their true identity. While some have *resolved* to consciously desire self-growth through personal assessment using their skills and competency to form an identity for their life. Others were *guided* to see themselves in a particular fashion built up under a parental cover that gave them a sense of identity. Many others are in total *neglect*, they don't care at all - as long as they survive; eat, drink and party, they just become whatever they settle for at the end.

Nobody can move from little to greatness without the crown of active consciousness. Take a peep into yesterday and its unfolding phase as children, young and innocent minds connected to our little world we barely understood anything, we danced and played our way to school; hunting into the woods of life we spread our wings carefree, curdled by the cares of attention we were pets, as the day went dark from the fall of morning light we watched the cloud arrayed with shining stars gazing into the heaven, the moon spread its light over our head, television beam flashed our wall with news, day and night, movies and games trilled our fantasies, as we shared funny stories by the hours until the night caught us to bed. Our childhood days: once upon a time, blazes of memory…See how time flies, a boy today a man tomorrow. The catch is, being a big boy or girl today doesn't mean you are awake to the facts of how things work. (This is how you find your advantage) know how things work.

CONSCIOUSNESS THROUGH THE BURDEN OF RESPONSIBILITY

Many of us were never taught the true value of our lives and how things truly work, left to chance, thus we burned the candles of each day as it fades into the shadows of eternity. We enjoyed the fun of the day until the demands of maturity come knocking, wake up boy, wake up girl it is day break. You knew that you have left your childhood days when you can distinguish the weight of a responsible mind and a playful mind. ***The day just broke for you when you understood the burden of responsibility. 'Responsibility shapes your sense of assessment through the role you play'***

WHERE DOES CONSCIOUSNESS MEET PURPOSE?

Every child is raised in a family like a flower watered with words and actions that formed our conscious mind over a period of time. As consciousness drives our understanding we learn and interact with our environment through observation, we become aware of our feelings, desires, taste, and worries sharing or participating in life changing moments with our families whether good or bad, formed our perception. These life sensational jiffies bring you to a point when self-consciousness sets in: we suddenly see the inward state of our hearts; our happiness, dislikes, resentment, emotions bubbling through our blood vessels and the outward facts about life that gawp our imagination daily. Yet in the echoes of these impelling activities nothing suggested purpose to us, oh! See how ignorance has rubbed us? I guess as much my friend.

People generally wake up every day to pursue their daily incomes, drove through the traffic huddles of the city, enjoyed the flare of party beats, participated in community services, drawn into a triangle of love out of the ordinariness of life flipping activities, overcome by the attraction and the happiness it brought: they married and settled for a life they knew little about. *It will surprise you to know that many adults today do not have a clue or an insight about their life's purpose.* **Purpose gives identity and identity brings purpose.** Existence without the awaken touch of purpose leave men in puzzle land, alive but clueless. Adulthood gave many a quest for life's "ambition" but little about purpose. **Destiny is a journey of purpose and fulfilling it.**

Your purpose for living is predetermined before you got here. Note: every Creator knows the purpose of its creature or product. Therefore, purpose must be discovered. It is purpose that gives you the consciousness of God and the revelation of why you were put together. ***It is the discovery of purpose that gives men the true light of perception. Your greatness is in your purpose and the fulfilment of your assignment.*** Many children enjoyed good cloths and many are being clothed in fine purples without the training of purpose.

CONSCIOUSNESS THROUGH THE VOICE OF REASONING

Who truly listens to the voice of 'reason' in the midst of countless opportunities and the struggle to fit in? When we float in the boat of merriment happy-go-lucky led by the freedom of our choices, until the storms of life and adversity comes - prompt by the call of life and the awakening moment that follows. Suddenly, the heart searches for meaning closely and seek for power to respond, if possible changes certain events we feel bitter about…awake to time and our pressing needs, the heart ponders in the sea of many questions and in the flood of pains. Then you wonder *what does my life count for really?* It takes a degree of consciousness to live a life of purpose.

Am I just another number in my house/another number born out of the touch of love by my parents, or just another number in the world's population record? Pondering... the mind is held to a pause searching for answers. You are not just a number in a census count, a piece of statistic in a data collection by your national government or a state property. No, *you are a person with meaning and purpose for existence.* Awake! to your state of mind and the shape of your world as it is; testing the waters of truth you wish you knew better, brushed against the boundaries of your space, tuned to this world called the circle of time you have a life to live, find your purpose now.

How does purpose enhances our life? A man awake to his purpose enjoys firmness and dedicated existence. *The best of life is stored in your identity of purpose, Creating a life outside the path of purpose is failing without knowing.* It makes you take control of your life in the right direction. *Purpose is our unique brand of identity.* It gives you strength beyond the physical to do the impossible. *Purpose drives your abilities to greatness.*

BE CONSCIOUS OF THESE 6 LAYERS OF YOUR ABILITIES AND THE DYNAMICS OF OPPORTUNITY.

1. **Personal strengths**: what do I have that makes me unique from my peers? What do I do easily without any formal training? What is my talent and natural endowment? Developing and exercising your personal strength is an essential aspect of personal growth, awareness and development. Ultimately you want to be happy and able to make your life work for you. Sometimes you don't know how good you are until you experience or confront some difficulties, exposures, friends and environment. Developing your strength to full potency is a journey. Taking your talent and strength to provide service and solutions create opportunity for success. *Build a market of profitable demand around your area of strength.*
2. **People Skills**: understanding people is the art of life. It begins

connect to people, finding and meeting the right people and keeping them when you find them is one layer of strength you must consciously develop. *Miss treating people is loosing opportunities without knowing.*

3. **Critical thinking skills**: our ability to rise out of our current position to our desired destination depends on critical thinking. Being able to carefully examine something, identify a problem or the situation as well as the factors that may influence it and being able to develop a course of actions well thought out with creativity. So you identify the problem, gather information, evaluate the evidence, consider solutions and choose and implement. *You must learn how to think for yourself and attract good opportunities to yourself.*

4. **Life skills**: to be able to deal with the events and challenges of life with focus and self-control you need these life skills. Self-awareness, creative thinking, decision making, effective communication, interpersonal relationship, active listening skills, networking and self-management. Get better with daily improvement in the area you need the most. ***Ask yourself what profitable skill can I develop to earn economic value for myself? What money skills have I learnt that can put 10,000 dollars and above in my pocket monthly? What skill have I acquired in the last five years that can position me for future advantages and minimize future shocks?*** Your goals should tell you which area of skill to develop.

5. **Education**: is not all about learning how to read and write or developing a core area of competence by acquiring a certificate to be employable. It also your ability to source for information, ideas, people and resources and apply them for wealth creation and life transformation. Most people have class room education but lack life education on finances, marriage, and others life essential skills. *The goal of education is to make you resourceful and productive.*

6. **Business know-how**: is required for everyday success, understanding how to serve your market with your gift, talents, product and services generating a system of profits not a onetime profit from a transaction is vital. It is easy to start a business but it requires skills to manage it. You must learn how to identify local resources and the market opportunities around you. What do people need around me that I can provide or which market is currently underserved? Identifying an opportunity, growing it and sustaining it for future wherewithal and relevance are business know-how. *Life is an interaction of business needs and the man with the right solution and system of advantage wins the gold.*
 Fulfilment is the outcome of a life lead by purpose using your abilities to your advantage.

NEVER JUDGE YOUR PURPOSE OR ABILITY BY THE CONDITION OF YOUR BIRTH Out of the versed flow of humanity; the entire human race, culture, colours and the nations of this world? Yes. You were born into a family whether big or small, noble or great, royal or presidential, in the cave or in the hospital, in the jungle or in the city, poor or rich. You may not even like the story surrounding your birth circumstance, ignore how you came in and pursue why you are here.

Birthday is a common experience for all men. You had a beginning; a product of love or a careless affair, a product of lust induced by seduction of the mind or alcohol, born out of wedlock, a perceived mistake to the one who gave birth to you, or born by two married couples shaded by the moon of love, flowered by the bond of beauty who cherished you or born out of the worst condition possible. Whatever the realities surrounding your birth – no matter what the story is, celebrate it. *How or where you were born does not change your purpose for existence.* **Life is always empty of substance without the joy of purpose irrespective of how and where you were born.**

The people in your life help to form your perception whether you know it or not. Sooner or later you will consciously and unconsciously mirror what they believed in, their fears, strength, wealth attitude or poverty mind-set, their abilities and in-abilities. Seeing life base on the choice they make and their thinking pattern or the things they allow, you begin to form a personality type, developing life concept of your own discernment. ***All men live according to their conscious desires.***

The revelation of purpose most time is acquired in moments of life changing seasons as you gain directives from God in prayers, you begin to articulate purpose through; the pains of your experience, your unique gift or talent, your core desires that pushes the button of your curiosity, the need that sparks your creativity, the human cries and crises that you cannot ignore responding to, the things that form your core interest: like the passion to heal, deliver, create and things you love to do. - Your unique design. You are designed with special abilities both physical and spiritual that reveal what you are equipped with for effective living. Your desires to do certain things that promote effective living show what is coded into your design to function and apply your mind to work. Once you begin to express what you are designed to do, you are living purpose. ***What are you designed and destined to do? One conscious answer will reveal your purpose.***

BE INSPIRED BY YOUR OWN STRUGGLE.

Let the purpose behind your birth inspire you to greatness. Most great men had little beginning and could not even predict their future. They face trying times that almost crippled their vision yet they refused to quit and did not allow the thoughts of hopelessness to trap them down, but rose to prominence with one conscious act at a time only to wake up with gold to share.

I wonder if your cognitive ability has driven you to grief or exploit. *Your ability to think, understand, learn and remember things forms your conscious mind.* Thinking the right thoughts is the only way to live the right life. When your understanding is 'poor', it affects your perception and your actions poorly. Learning is a deliberate action to gain knowledge or skill by studying, practicing, being taught, or experiencing something. Acquire only the right knowledge that can enhance your purpose. ***The best lessons of life are not taught, there are deduced.*** You must learn how to use logic or reason to form conclusions about the things going on in your life: to decide something after thinking about the known facts. *Those who do not remember their mistakes in the past repeat them over and over again falling to a common enemy.*

What are the enemies of your purpose? *Whatever you fail to discover you will fail to maximise and the enemy you fail to overcome, will do you more harm than good.* 'The enemies of your purpose are the biggest threat to your successful existence'. Do identify them because it is a straightforward requirement for success. Information is only useful when you remember them. *Without the consciousness of our purpose, men will live without exploit to share.* Whatever you sow into your consciousness is the bedrock of all achievement. *Careless existence ends when a man gains the consciousness of his purpose.*

CHAPTER 4

WHO ARE YOU TO THINK BIG?

Every second that you are alive, you are spending a piece of your thought pattern and a piece of the purpose that drives you.

Life is an investment of thoughts. Thoughts are derived dynamic energy: words, information, pictures and concepts of ideas with life giving force applicable to time, to create, destroy, design, build, conform and transform. Every thought have its source of influence. Thoughts are seeds with life and power of their own, conceived in the mind through understanding and imagination. They are developed in the heart through belief and feelings, and expressed through the body. Your mind is the door of imagination for creative adventures or the birthing place of success. **Whatever is creating your thinking pattern will gain strong control over your life.** Knowing what and how to think: developing corresponding actions is the primary key to mastery. Your life will be the expression of your thinking, the interpretation of your actions and the reflections of your desires. *Directing your mind in an effective and consistent fashion through meditation, contemplation and reflection is crowning the champion in you.*

Are you clear about the 20% of the things you think about daily and the 80% outcomes of your thought habits? Your thoughts habits are your strong holds or your predilection. If nothing changes in your thinking pattern in the next five years, you will remain the same person you are in character, identity and results. You will always reap the fruit of your thought investment. Therefore, you must adopt the mind-set of a business investor to generate specific results. Investor's think in terms of profit, return on investment both short and long time bases using measurable indicators, timing and due diligence in all they do to protect against foreseeable loses. Note: only poor investors live with poor results. You cannot produce 'balance' in your life when your thinking is out of balance.

If you don't grow big in your thinking, your height or age will not matter. *An uncoordinated thought process will produce unstable lifestyle.* Once you have a critical or analytical improvement in your thought process, you will see dramatic improvement in all you do. 80% of the results you will attain in life will come from the failure or success of investing the right 20% of strategic clear thinking. Life splendour is formed in moments of clear thinking, decision making, choice, goal setting, and actions. *Consider this*; human achievements relating to height, depth, length, quantity, quality and results are functions of our thinking. *Your life will turn out directly after the image of your mind.* You may not become all you can think about, but you cannot animate the life your mind cannot conceive or apprehend.

It is the Renaissance artist, **Michelangelo Buonarroti** that said: *"the greatest danger for most of us is not that our aim is too high and we miss it, but that it is too low and we reach it"*. People do not think big or cannot aim high enough because they are afraid they might fail; low self-esteem, poor belief system, not willing to step out their comfort zone, tied down by other people opinions about them and the lack of strength to go the extra mile. Moreover, the negative forces of life that possesses human being often threaten the success of big thinkers because they want to reduce them to the level they are comfortable with, just to feel secure and less intimidated. (Do not let anything reduce you into the image size of their imagination for you) see, people do not hit new heights by accident: think up and you will go up. You must have a clear picture first.

When your thoughts are not clear to you, your actions will not be clear, your expectations will not be clear either and your life direction will not be clear to you.

It is the size of your thinking that affects the size of your world. Whatever you think about will show up in your life eventually. Whatsoever you think on is the catalyst substance for action and results. Who are you to think big is life most interesting question you will ever get to answer. *Who you are and what you think about has a corresponding effect on destiny: knowing the difference is principal knowledge.* It is not all about what you think but who you become at *rise to the level of your thought pattern.* You create new beginnings by forming new thoughts toward a meaningful cause or course. (Cause = foundation and course = progression) Your thoughts are causes and rewards are effects.

A mind empty of substance equals a void life. ***Nothing is too small or too big for the mind to conceive.*** For those people who think you can't amount to anything big should wait and see.

It is not people opinion about you that determines how you turn out, but the power in your choice that transforms your potentials into charming and mind boggling results. Be careful what you call impossible. *"It always seems impossible until it's done."* - **Nelson Mandela.** Believe me until you doubt your greatness, you are greatness in the making. The question is how great do you want to be? Whatever you think on the most on the level of your belief system is what you will become. Your world begins to change as you think better and employ time well as a resourceful time manager. ***Concentrated thinking gives you navigation abilities.*** Practise it until you master it.

Understanding your purpose for existence enlightens and disciplines your course of action because *purpose is the creative power of destiny.* ***The loss of purpose is bigger than the loss of time.*** Time can only be valued by the purpose you are. Therefore, a life empty of purpose is like a car without a driver, when purpose engages time, energy becomes resources. ***A man is not qualified to be alive without a meaning for his life.*** A man without a clear purpose for life gropes in the dark, living a life of emptiness, coping never planning, easily lost, with a permanent wondering mind about what to do with time. Those people who can't find their unique purpose for living join the crowd heading nowhere without knowing their place and calling in life.

Clarity is power: you were designed to be a solution, to fill a particular need in life, solve a particular problem in your immediate environment and beyond. You cannot serve your world well by being a problem or a nuisance. The world needs you; there is something in you that you can tap into; an invention, an idea, an innovation or a solution that will be the key to your next level in life. *If you think above your current environment, you will rise above it eventually.* "Greatness is in the seed of ideas: develop the right one". **Great people are men or women with the capacity to generate economic values or fruit that makes their generation depend on them.** Make your life a source of something great. *The reward for positive thinking is that, you will have a positive life to share.* Leave nothing to chance; it is the common act of failures. Your life will move consistently toward the dominant area of your thought. Therefore, think greatness, possibilities and success. Negative thinking carries destructive powers, root them out.

YOU ARE BORN TO BE GREAT.

Responsibility is the prize for greatness. Can every man become great if given the same opportunity? I wonder what the answer might be…sometimes people don't realise how fortunate they are until they experience the other side of life. The answer could be yes, or no depending on the individual. Some people wish that their lives will turn out great, well start working because; great men and women are not just born to be great, 'no' they all rise to the occasion. Therefore, *it is my opinion that every man is equipped with the power to become great.* Change is the only constant thing in life; believe in it because one change of event can lead to a big turn in your life. Adjusting and responding to forces outside your influence have a substantial impact on your destiny.

Don't die for what you lack today instead make the most of what you have, until you hit your set target. *Great people only ask one question which is, is it possible?* "Everything is possible to him that believes" – **the Bible.** *Believe it until you make it.* It was **Zig Ziglar** that said: *"the best thing about the future is that it comes only one day at a time."* Therefore, you can't experience total change at a time. *If you let people define what is possible for you before you challenge yourself to rise out of the dust of mediocrity and average living, then you have*

Never dream for accidental success. You may wait too long because nothing happen by accident.

CAPACITY CHANGES EVERYTHING.

Are you capable of effecting the change you desperately need? Are you equipped to 'facilitate' your plans to fruition in your present circumstance? *A man that has a plan has a future, but a man with capacity rules the moment.* If you are incapable of making progress now, the reason is fear has buried your strength and courage. It is not age or height or your size that determines your capacity. ***It is your ability to do something that counts: a mental, emotional and physical ability.*** Your mind is the key to unlocking your world, when a mind is broken down in weak thoughts, abuses, struggling mentality and negative inputs; it becomes increasingly difficult to produce transformation except it is corrected with new images, new information and new facts. Except that mind begins to picture new possibilities, act on new information and structural facts, it is crippled in itself to produce life of its own. *Emotional stability is fundamental in navigating through life ever changing realities.*

There are emotional bondages and traps that can keep people down permanently - hurt beyond repair, living with the bitterness of yesterday's misfortunes, too attached to sentiments that are irrelevant to rise above it and the inability to forgive and move on. Throw your emotional baggage away by replacing them with words that will challenge you to achieve more like; I can do it irrespective of how I fell. 'Do not let your temperament, condition you into a failure'. ***Every man is equipped with unique abilities in them to produce their desired effect.*** Dig deep and find yours. Whenever you begin to despise your own ability to achieve greatness you don't need an opposition because you are self-opposing.

You will begin to lose confidence dramatically counting the emptiness in your life, but when you say, there is more to my life that I can see now, you stand up for yourself to improve and embrace growth. When you say I can make my life work with God on my side, what do I need to know? You begin to "attract" the right knowledge, people, opportunities and you set yourself up for success. **Remember this for life; your thinking is an attraction trigger. Whatever you want in your life now, can be pulled to you by practising "attraction thinking".**

The action or power of evoking interest, pleasure, or liking for someone or something: the power of drawing forth a response from people that matters by appealing to their desires and taste, ego and strength. When people are attracted to you, they favour you and whatever you are attracted to you magnetise. **Those who make the right attraction circle command powerful effects.** # *Spark your flame of creativity to burn because creative mind has enough capacity to change anything.* A mind opened to new ideas finds new concepts and strategy for progress. Find time to do this often, laugh and rejoice over your struggles and victories, it will bring you emotional healing and peace of mind.

If nothing weighs you down, you cannot stay down. *Every man is capable inside except when the mind of the individual sees a different picture. What you see about yourself becomes your reality.* Note: difficulties are part of life experience; hence your ability to navigate through life's difficulties is central to becoming a champion. A man dressed in weak thoughts becomes a victim while a mind clothed with inner strength knocks down opposition and clinch victory when it matters. It takes capacity to knock down opposition.

BEAT THE ODDS

Victory begins when you pursue excellence. Be the best in what you do and you will be in front. Children nurtured for excellence always rise to the position of excellence. If you miss the age of parental nurturing, do well to gain the act of preparation and win big. There is no quality you lack today that cannot be acquired through precise decision. *Make no excuse for failure only employ the act of preparation for everything you need, because success is the best revenge on yesterday's failure.* Champions prepare adequately to seize their opportunities: please put your life in the right context now, because prepared fighters with the right strategy take victory home.

THE ACT OF PREPARATION AND EXCELLENCE

P – PLAN AND PLAY TO WIN

R – REACH FOR TOOLS

E – EMPLOY TIME WISELY

P – PUSH TO THE LIMIT

A – ACQUIRE STRATEGY

R – REVIEW YOUR ACTIONS

A – ACT LIKE IT

T – TACKLE YOUR WEAKNESS

I – INCREASE YOUR CAPACITY

O – ORGANISE

N – NETWORK

Uncertainty most time marks the events of the day, live up to it. Living in an uncertain world requires a great deal of preparation to engage it without too many regrets. Don't fear failure! Fear being in the exact same place next year as you are today without any significant change of position. A man will remain in a fixed position until he acquires principal knowledge. It is **Brain Tracy** that said: *knowledge is power, but only knowledge that can be applied to practical purpose in some way.* ***You lack nothing in life until you lack creative steps coordinated by knowledge.***

PLAN AND PLAY TO WIN

Every human need reveals our ability to search out ways to fulfil it. A man with a gratifying need is a man that can produce a plan; it takes a need to create a plan. Therefore, failure to plan is planning to fail. To achieve your set objective, you must create a plan worthy of pursuing it. Set a clear direction for the day before you end it, because a successful day will unfold a successful week progressively. What must I achieve today? ***Each day has a benefit to offer, why loose it to lack of a strong plan?*** Write it down, count the cost and go to work. While you work, play to win with integrity, play with diligence, good cooperation and with a healthy attitude. Avoid unnecessary conflict, avoid distractions and avoid associations that will undermine your success. Cutting corners will cut you short, play your card with a win-win hand of trust and stay dependable.

REACH FOR TOOLS

Equip your mind with the right tools and you will rule your circumstance. ***A man without the right tool for success is a handicap.*** All height is attainable if you are equipped to attain it. It is dis-service to wait for somebody to make your life work for you. Build your ability up consistently to meet the demand of your destiny. Ask yourself this question, am I equipped to succeed with my current level of skills, knowledge and resources? Make no wrong assumption about the tools you require to making your life count.

EMPLOY TIME WISELY

The mastery of time is beginning of all mastery. People seldom plan the use of their time because they have low Expectations about themselves. What you do with your time is the future you are waiting for. If you measure your hours effectively, you will control your minutes meaningfully. The time you gain today is capital for future advantage. Those who approach the day without a specific target run in unfortunate circles. Those who gain time, think forward before acting forward. ***Time is Empty of value without the drive of focus.***

"*There may be a thousand little choice in a day, all of them count.*" - **Shad Helmstetter.** Make your time count. Time can't tell you what the future holds, but how you address it or how you engage it becomes your future. If nobody pays you after twenty-four hours consistently in one month, you are practicing poverty. *Value commands the chain of wealth.* Billionaires don't live with extra time: they only distribute extra value. Become a wise time manager and eliminate time abusers out of your daily schedules.

PUSH TO THE LIMIT

Life circumstances will stretch your mind and ability to stay in the fight and in the race of life, you must push to the limit of your own fear and courage. Persistence and determination will keep you going through trying times and dark nights. Do not give up; do not give in until you win. Winners don't quit and quitters don't win. Accept inconvenience for the sake of your dream; see pain as a tool not a burden. When you fill like quitting, resolve for new heights, finish the task at hand because there is a joy of fulfilment waiting.

ACQUIRE STRATEGY

Strategic thinking births new possibilities. Do not see the road blocks along your path and permit them to stop you from moving forward. Create a blueprint to your desired destination with a depth of details to lead forward. Strategy is the game of the wise.

REVIEW YOUR ACTION.

Review your action steps as you make a countdown to your dream land. Avoid pitfalls along the way that could compromise your ability to reach your destination. Make a daily review or a weekly review of progress made. Ask yourself if I continue to do the things I'm doing now over and over again, will it help me to achieve my goal? Do a performance test to check for any inconsistent activity dragging you behind and sustain activities consistent with your set direction.

ACT LIKE IT.

It is true that thinking affects living. The key to a fruitful existence is in the seat of your imagination. Create a perfect image of your ideal person and hold that long enough to allow it affect the way you act and do things. Talk, walk, play and work like you're already in your dream land. When you picture yourself poor, weak, incapable, deprived, you hardly think positive thoughts which will ultimately affect the way you see yourself. ***How you see yourself affects the way you think and act.*** Perception affects performance. Act it until you make it.

TACKLE YOUR WEAKNESS

It is easy to think that you don't have any weakness in your life. **One hidden and undiscovered weakness can trap a person in permanent circle of struggles.** Your weakness is your worst trap – address them effectively. When you discover your weakness, don't excuse it away but, if you have an obvious weakness limiting your ability to handle life, don't beat yourself down with words like, 'I'm not good enough'; 'I can't make it'. Don't let any particular weakness stop you ever. If you have failed before, now is your chance to succeed. Get help from the appropriate quarter necessary, a coach and a counsellor to help improve your ability to handle your weaknesses and overcome them. Identify the possible trigger for this weakness in your life before you decide on a solution. Caution: you may not overcome all your weaknesses overnight. It is possible to have a recurrent relapse of the things you wish you never revisit. Keep your focus until you stand on your two feet.

INCREASE YOUR CAPACITY

Competent people take the lead in life. *"The future belongs to the competent, get good, get better, be the best!"* – **Brain Tracy.** Becoming competent should be your top priority in life, polish your ability in every area to be able to stand out in all you do. You are a star waiting to shine, equipped with all it takes in becoming the best. You can develop yourself to lead, deliver result and achieve uncommon feat in life. Don't let the lack of means be your obstacle because where there is a will, there is a way.

ORGANISE YOURSELF

Organization leads to personal and institutional efficiency. Take control of everything out of balance in your life and eliminate your flaws. The underlying factor for mediocrity and failures is the lack of organizational skill. Where everything goes: you easily lose control of your time and your life. Cut your loose ends and shape a lifestyle that allows you to build a sustainable life.

NETWORK

Evaluate every person in your life now and weigh their impact on you so far, do yourself a favour to connect with highly effective people that can boost your chance of succeeding. Travelling with the wrong crowd will only produce a negative drag. *'Life is a network of association'* Feel free to approach the man or woman of your dream, get a recommendation, write them or make a courtesy visit and establish contact with them, let them inspire, motivate and mentor you. In cases where physical contact is difficult, get their books, link with them online or get to call them. Whoever challenges you to reach for more and to be a better person is a good person to stay connected to. Can you be that person for others and help to shape their destiny? It is iron that sharpens iron, quality people attract like-minded people. Once you disconnect from old friends that can potentially hamper your growth, expect some negative reactions from them. However, use diplomacy to handle them as you simply state the need for the changes you are making in your life now and watch how they adjust and cooperate with you.

CHAPTER 5
WHAT IS ACCOMPLISHMENT FOR YOU?
You are a success in progress equipped beyond any reasonable doubt.

The path of success is for all, it is not for the exclusive minority of the society. Exercising your strength as a possible achiever is anchored on your selective choice as an individual because you have principally to a certain degree abilities to control the outcomes of your life. *A man must make profitable decisions and solve his problems to push himself to any height of success, allowing doubts to program your steps is fatal to success.* Whenever you doubt your ability and your chances to make it, you lose the self-confidence to articulate your steps towards your greatest goal. The realization that much of whatever I become in life is centred on the things I do or fail to do, free you from the feeling of being trapped in time.

Certain things will happen to you that will not align to your expectations plotting your destiny path. Therefore, worry less about the things you cannot control and take charge of all you can. If you are waiting for a twist of fate to determine your personal life outcome, you lose the concentration and ability to plan ahead. Only wishful thinkers live in procrastination land. Never be afraid to think big, set high attainable goals, and then summon the courage to pursue them. *You don't need the cooperation of everybody to make it, just the right partnership or contacts. Locate them.* At the end, what do you really want to accomplish in life? What kind of a man or woman do I want to be? Seeing the finish line ahead of time reminds you of why you can't fail until the successful completion of your set objective. *Work is the secret of achievers, are you ready to work?* **Diligent and smart work with steady growth will bring you accomplishment.** If you want to be remembered for something, then you must stand up for something big.

SEE YOUR LIFE IN FULL CIRCLE

Living a balance and fulfilled life with peace of mind to share is the biggest accomplishment in life. What kind of partner do you want to be? How healthy do you want be at 70? What kind of business system do you want to build? What kind of father or mother do you want to be? What kind of working environment are you building for the next generation? What kind of friend do you want to be? You must create a vivid destiny path to follow with a balanced approach to it. *What role do you play in life?* A leader, husband, mother, sports player, colleague, team member, teacher, coach, whatever be the role you play, what will be your accomplishment? Which areas of life are more important to you, where you must contribute to enhance the global position of your country? Assess each area carefully knowing that your happiness and fulfilment depends on your accomplishment.

STAND AND LEAD

Vision is the secret of great achievers, a clear direction of where you're going and how to get there. Visionary actions produce leaders, but you can't lead others until you lead yourself well. **Leading yourself well is the first task for accomplishment.** It takes ambitious, self-disciplined individuals with a calculated focus to flourish and accomplish meaningful land shaking results. Men of vision do a lot of personal sacrifice and delay gratification to complete a worthy course. If you see the ultimate, you can overcome the immediate. Vision produces a sense of mission and your life assignment conditions discipline. A disciplined person develops a sense of direction and a mission for living, and prepares for uncommon accomplishment. *Discipline shapes your ability to lead yourself without supervision. Without the life of discipline, a cheap fall is near. Discipline is the evidence of a solid Character.*

There is always a price to pay on your way to success. *So why is it that people don't accomplish much?* Primarily, it is because of the lack of vision, the chains of fear, inferiority complex, laziness and zero motivation amidst other things that hinders people from accomplishing much. The environment you come from can be a factor, your inability to dream big and aim higher in life, living in poverty can lowers an individual expectation to think big about anything, parents with low income to support their children's dream hamper their strength to believe for something big or even try.

Some have abused and mismanaged their privileges; some are buried in the shadows of their parents not able to ever stand out on their own, while some are trapped in bad habits that have and can ruin their chances of accomplishing anything worthwhile. Money is a key element in all you want to do and the lack of it is very frustrating. **"There is always a money solution when you settle down to find one".** The easier you achieve economic growth the better your odds of accomplishing something big.

THE MISSING LINK

What the environment you live in today lack, is you. Wow! How can I believe that? Hoping that it will get better without any meaningful input is just wishful thinking. Can the world be better because of you? Ponder it a little. *The greatness in us is most time covered in the limitations we face and the ones we permit to stand.* Know your limitations and overcome them. Put your mind to work because it is the bedrock of industry, civilization, inventions and economic revolution. Eighty per cent of the wealth you seek lies within your imagination and your ability to produce value; the other twenty per cent will come from the quality people in your life. ***The wealthiest place is the bank of the mind.*** You may never live in a world without a problem; they actually exist to be solved. More so, there are opportunities for you to thrive on. ***Every great mind produces great solutions - don't die poor.*** "The future you must direct". A man without a growth pattern will end up with struggling patterns.

Deal with your boundaries: what are the boundaries you have accepted without knowing? *The heart can't push down boundaries the mind hasn't conquered. Boundaries are limited thoughts conceived.* Have you concluded that this wealthy life is not for me; I can't just see myself making it? Be careful, and watch the ideas you allow to govern your mind. *Whatever cripples your thinking and your ability to* mountain you can't conquer whether perceived or real.

A man beaten in his perception lost seven times before the battle even began, men don't fall in battles for the lack of sword, but they are ambushed by their own fear. Fear is not what you see, but what you perceive. **The wrong perception of a situation is more dangerous than the situation itself. Therefore, a faulty perception will lead to an incorrect conclusion.** *Man is a child of his perception in the pool of his realities.* Break those perceived boundaries now and show others the way. *"If your actions inspire others to dream more, learn more, do more and become more, you are a leader."* - **John Quincy Adams**

Deal with your inheritance: parents transfer both strength and weakness to their children. You have one to deal with. If you let your parent's inabilities stop you from accomplishing something gigantic in life, then you have settled for mediocrity. Whether you have a weak or strong background, the key you need is knowledge, wisdom and understanding. Inspire yourself and find a beginning point for you, quit looking for who will come and rescue you. Do not put or rest your destiny on the shoulders of anyone because it is a sign of weakness. *Do not frighten yourself with the distance between where you are now and your desired destination.* Wear-off all oppositions, be a man on the goal even when you doubt yourself, step out, forward only and double your chance of succeeding. Fight your fears until you win. See you at the top.

YES YOU CAN!

You can triumph and accomplish the perceived impossible task, by embracing the challenge and becoming efficient in all you do: equip your mind thoroughly with the mind-set of an achiever. There is no apparatus now that we can use to measure what accomplishment is for you. Accomplish simply means: to succeed in doing (something positively impactful) to bring about a result by effort and to bring to completion a set task. *Fulfilment is the joy of achievers that breathe of celebration that shows that you are satisfied.* **You must learn of necessity, how to put to effect or execute your action plans, in a**

successful progression to bring to fruition your desired dream.

This special skill or ability is gained by practice and good training. (The act of accomplishing) once you learn how to complete your project well, you add a feather to your cap. *Be a project manager per excellence.* A man is accomplished when he can provide for his family adequately. A man is also accomplished when he is established in his work or business with a good and sustainable cash flow. A man is said to be accomplished when the return on his investments and life time labour is now yielding dividends that surpass his annual expenses yearly.

You are accomplished when your children are stars in their respective field living fulfilled because of you. A man is accomplished when his worship and commitment to God is total with zero money distraction. A man is fulfilled when his family is enjoying total peace and harmony. A man is also fulfilled when he can make significant contribution to his community and help others grow and succeed in life. *The road to self-accomplishment is task driven and long. Keep at it until you make it.*

CHAPTER 6

LAYING THE RIGHT FOUNDATION

Everything hangs in a balance where habit is DISFUNCTIONAL. A habit formed is a life formed: whether bad or good ones.

It is true that your life is a direct reflection of your habitual lifestyle. Whether you like it or not you have a habit pattern that can either make or break you. The underlying force for success is habit. **Your habit is who you are.** You set your own height in life when you redefine your habits. Every habit you form has a potential consequence; it becomes the foundation on which you build on. **Winning habits make winners and the opposite is true.** Whatever you do consistently in an excellent fashion with an outstanding result boosts your self-image and self-worth.

IT IS IN THE ROOT

How do I form the habit that is consistent with my vision or pursuit? I once read a material that revealed these basic principles of how we form our 'habits and characters'. *Sow the seed of thought and you will reap an action, sow an action and reap habit, sow a habit and you will reap a character, sow a character and reap a destiny.* The most important aspect of your life is the thinking pattern or the concept of thought you have conceived and accepted. Could it be that, all you have believed about your life is fundamentally wrong? Ideas matter, because they can govern and rule your life. Whenever you think impossible thoughts, they gradually take root in you without warning so much that you act unconsciously the failures in your mind.

Even when you gain opportunity for a breakthrough out of your situation you immediately sabotage your success without knowing because the negative is now governing your life in the mist of opportunities. *If your mind has created poverty thinking for you, no amount of money can make you rich.* Therefore, if you think lack, you experience lack. Your thought pattern drives your life events and outcomes: nurture the right ones. Tap into new roots of information consistent with your ideals and see the transformation.

Forming the right thinking pattern is all you need to create a new life because the subconscious mind is a faithful servant that accepts all programing data. *"Above all else, Guard your heart, for it is the wellspring of life"* – **Proverbs 4:23.** The results of your life will only spring from the state of your heart or your mind. Whatever goes into your heart will come out of your life. *Your heart is designed to believe the information it perceives to be true.* Who told you, that you are poor, you are nobody, you can't make it, that level is impossible for you, you've lost it all, is too late now…..? People believe what they want to believe but blame others for their results. When I told you that you are a star per excellence I meant it. ***The heart is the most fragile seat of intelligence: you must guide it.***

G.U.A.R.D means G – gather resourceful information. U – Utilize it adequately. A – Articulate the facts. R – Reject false information. D – Develop and deploy new and relevant information. Whenever you gather the right information it guides you from possible errors, mistakes and misconceptions. Your sense for discernment and ability to interpret information becomes sharper and your ability to utilize information adequately is strengthened where your investigative mind is empowered. At this point, your understanding is deepened to see clearly, connecting facts to facts, which enables you to say no to false information and finally cultivate the sense to develop personal concepts and ideas that are consistent with the truth even with the capacity to deploy and apply key information. Whenever people give-in and accept information cheaply and blindly without any intelligent debate, analysis and logical consideration, they have not yet formed their GUARD intelligence.

ACTION

A person cannot act above his level of knowledge per time. You can predict a man's future by just the way he acts. One popular adage says that, 'action speaks louder than words'. Why is that? It is so because action reflects or exposes the state of our emotions or the state of minds. Therefore, a man who wants to succeed must locate success *action produces no result.* ***Whatever you do consistently long enough becomes your habit.*** Weigh your actions now by predicting your own future. Look carefully on the action steps of great men and women, they only do the relevant and pursue their set goals until it is achieved. If your actions don't betray you nobody can. Act with the mentality of a champion, those who act forward stay forward.

HABIT

The prevailing disposition or character of a person's thoughts and feelings is his/her mental makeup. The manners of conducting oneself: a behaviour pattern acquired by frequent repetition or physiologic exposure that shows itself in a regular or increased facility of performance, an acquired mode of behaviour that has become nearly or completely involuntary. What is your mental make-up? The things you believe in are a key part of your mental make-up. Whatever you believe is true for you becomes your reality. Consider this thought; *"It's not what a man knows that hurts him; it's what he knows that isn't TRUE."* - **Josh Billings.**

When you form a behaviour pattern based on false information it rules your life until you encounter a new light that delivers you from the chains of your mind. The belief system you have created forms a major part of your habits and manners, what you can do and the things you can't do. Unlearn old belief systems that are not consistent with your future desire as you begin to make new confession repeatedly to allow you form new thinking configuration. If you were failing before now, do this every morning; I am a man of excellence, a success in progress, I couldn't fail even if I try, the days of failure are over, I have good credit for my labour, my mind is sharp for comprehension and understanding, and I will end in flying colours.

"Every word spoken to you forms an attitude in your mind and a disposition towards that person". Everybody acts according to the word deposit in them. Whatever is your experience today in life, note; *good confession will produce good reasoning, good feelings, good actions, good habit, good character and a good outcome.* The

opposite is true. **Words are the building blocks of habits.** Watch who influences your life because they are moulding your habits, that is why association affects absorption. Evil communication will always corrupt good manners and good communication will correct bad manners.

Build a man the right character in him, you have given him the world, and give him wisdom he will rule his world. Man's biggest problem is not ignorance, but refusal to see it or address it. *Bad character is a destiny destroyer.* Don't fight a man that lacks character, he has already taken a journey towards a fall. *'Reflect on your habits'.* People out of ignorance have destroy their relationship because of bad character, wrecked business opportunity, close doors of breakthrough all because of character flaws rooted in their mind. Do a personal evaluation today and locate character traits that can sabotage your destiny. *One significant change in character can make a big difference in your life.*

Character is the pillar of destiny, build the right one now. The knowledge you possess is the character of your person. 70% of a person's character is defined by his or her choice. You are one choice away from creating a new life. *Distinction is the mark of character; our character is the strongest unit of our personality.* Men with questionable habits lose opportunity easily. *Decision models the future but character sustains it.*

CHAPTER 7

WINNING INSTINCT THAT MAKES A CHAMPION.

There is no secret formula for learning to listen to your instincts –
T. D. Jakes

Instinct is a way of behaving, thinking or feeling that is not learned: a natural desire or tendency that makes you want to act in a particular way. It is something you know without learning it or thinking about it. Instinct is like a bearing handle in men that help them see, access and maximise their potentials, opportunities and resources around them in an ever changing world. Good instinct can make you a winner, a champion just by producing powerful actions through a nudge of internal reflexes.

Your ability to navigate through the complex seasons of your life: sense danger locking within close range, speculate or predict events with sharp astuteness, stepping into a strategic relationship instinctively, working with men and women of diverse backgrounds and can prefigure their tendencies seeing through conceal acts, locating opportunity in the face of difficulties, evolving into higher place of function as a leader, breaking free from a low level life, risking for critical change and maximising your inherent abilities and also, harnessing your external resources to live a more satisfying life on your trip to destiny through the vehicle of instinct. Living in a world full of surprises driven by high human energy and the mind field it embodies you must of necessity have an 'impulse drive' that makes you anticipate change, prepare for the unseen, seize opportunity quick, move out of the rut of life, innovate and lead from where you are to where you are going per time.

Men and women with instinctive abilities think better, faster, do the complex things of life with ease and work harder to bring about awesome and challenging results. Instinct as it were, being your ability to evolve from one stage to another, respond quickly to everything almost without thinking, generating solutions in a snap shot, avoid possible danger, protect and secure access to hidden fortune is beneficiary to all who will learn to listen to it. ***Instinctive***

thinking leads men into greatness and positions them in power. Sooner or later you will find yourself in a strategic position handling high demanding task or pressure from obvious lack in your life, that will trigger the release of instinctive thinking and abilities domicile in you.

Life crises, promotion into a high capacity job beyond your usual territory or level of comfort, economic limitations, the lack of life basic necessity, most times serve as catalyst in unravelling your instinct. There is no navigation system in the physical to tell you everything, what to do, when to, and how to respond in the face of difficulties, neither is there a system that provides answers to all of life questions when facing the inevitable, you will need more than intelligence to solve the issue facing you and to establish progress. There are times you will draw from the depth of your understanding, reasoning capacity and your ability to apply knowledge to manipulate one's environment listening to logic, instructions and facts "intelligence". *However, what do you do when your intelligence is not enough?*

Intellect by itself is limited. Please note that, instinct can be misapplied mostly when it is motivated by your immediate gratification, selfish gain at the expense of exploitation that satisfy without the check of conscience or thoughtful consideration of others. Instinct is not all about survival of the fittest - it is about knowing what to do instinctively out of the over-whelming realities of your situation to initiate growth, capitalize on your advantage, unlocking hidden treasures and opportunities that will profit many through you as the inspired channel. However, you can combine both intellect and instinct in an unusual fashion to advance and promote the quality of life around you. Instinct listens to the changes in the current wave of events and act accordingly while intellect makes you see the value in your action to secure profit. ***Intellect guides while instinct prompts.***

If you don't want to be buried in the ordinary, you must see the extra and think the extraordinary. You don't need a script to be productive; all you need is instinct to soar into the horizon of new possibilities.

Please don't waste your life doing the routine just to get by each day, instead rise to take on the challenge of becoming all you were designed to be. You can navigate from the maze of low-hanging opportunity to a place of fortune, wealth and abundance. The distance between what is, to what could be (your present struggle and your future prosperity) is always the longest distance known to the mind; when people begin to contemplate when will I ever make it? In the heat of uncertainty we doubt ourselves and our ability to grow above pressing circumstances, *but it is our creative propensity that drives us through the cloud of fear and uncertainty into our harbour of rest.*

It is T. D. Jakes that said; *"others can inspire you, but ultimately the only thing that empowers you is what lies within you and learning how to better utilize what you've been given"*. You've gotten all it takes, look inside. I have learnt from my personal experience that instinct can launch you from the back side of life to the front side of leadership and influence. Time may fail me to share with you all about my experiences, but you can take less and do more with it, turn a failing organization into a company of success, an impossible situation to others into a working miracle by the torch of instinct. Champions don't win by accident; they do so by instinct. Men of instinct are always sharp, quick and innovative. *If you have a need to grow and succeed fast activate your instinct!*

How do I harness, refine and apply my instinct in unlocking my doors to move from obscurity into prominence? Please understand that time and chance happen to all men as a window of opportunity that present itself in unique fashions for all. What you consider as pain, privation, and suffering is just a chance for you to respond instinctively. For example, Joseph the Hebrew boy, found himself before the king Pharaoh of Egypt to interpret his dream for him recommended by a fellow prisoner who has benefited from Joseph dream interpretation abilities led by a nudge of instinct. Note; ***"instinct is basically emotional signals and pointers in you"***. (Instinct listens to, and plugs into other people needs from a blind spot to others and stop at nothing but solution) interpreting Pharaoh's up giving the king a monumental advice that secured him a seat as the leader of his government in a foreign land. Why didn't he stop at the interpretation alone? Instant nudges of instinct obviously.

1. The key therefore, is in your ability to know that you were design to function well and equip with inherent instinctive abilities worthy of application that you can use it to navigate the map of destiny.
2. Understand the season and time you are in. A sense of timing and a nudge of impulse that helps take advantage of the moment.
3. Know when to take risk by your instinct in the midst of a doubtful situation. Risk is always a part of success equation because it takes risk to rise.
4. The willingness and the sensitivity to respond to your inner prompting.
5. Sharpen your observation and recognition skill to pick the difference in intervals, situations, locations, trend and people.
6. Learn to move and act quick base on instinct. Trying to over analyse all the facts before you act instinctively may end you losing your chance to the one who can act fast. Sometimes you do not need all the details at once; let them unfold as you travel.
7. Sharpen your ability to discern, identify and take advantage of opportunities when you see one, hidden to others. Finally, *do you want to fit-in or stand out? Let the instinct of a champion drive you to the finish line.*

CHAPTER 8

AVOID THE WAYS OF THE FOOLISH
*Foolishness support failure – **Dr Paul Enenche.***

The cup of foolishness and the bread of unwise actions are the manacles of a common man. *Could it be that your life would have been better if you were wiser*? Wisdom is priceless and it is a life requirement. *It is either you are spending the currency of wisdom or that of foolishness in running your life, there is no middle ground. One day of wisdom and another day of foolishness will only translate into an imbalance life.* Wisdom will always build men up while foolishness brings them down. It is not possible to live and not express one moment of foolishness or wisdom occasionally; however, living on the path of the foolish consistently is the sure way to imprison your greatness. The chains of foolishness bring men faster to their grave. *Foolhardiness evolves through a person's formative years, up to their adulthood.*

THE SUBTLE BEGINNING

Losing a child to life imprudence is the worst form of lost compared to the cost of time investment made into raising one? Yes it is. A man lost in the trap of foolishness subsists in the cage of misfortune. *Parent notice;* building a child's intellectual capacity to differentiate between a wise and a foolish decision is a capital requirement for their success. The truth is that, there is foolishness in every child growing up because they know less and think less about their actions. **Proverb 22:15** declares that, *"Foolishness is bound in the heart of a child; but the rod of correction shall drive it far from him"*. During these formative years of our lives, all we do is respond to calls and directions set by others. The mind at this age is too small to probe into motives whether good or bad, or make any intellectual assessment that is why - it is easy for people to mislead a child.

Most adults today were misled into certain things as children that have compromised their ability to function well in life. As we begin to mature under the watchful eyes of our parent, we learn and listen to their counsels benefiting from their pool of wisdom, experience and knowledge bank so much that, when we go wrong they help to correct, guide and shape us into who and what we are today. There is a tendency that parents can push their offspring's to the edge or put a great amount of pressure on them in an attempt to mold their lives according to their expectation for them. The tin line between child abuse and correction is "caution". A child should be given the position to reason and communicate their opinion sometimes. Whether they make sense or not in a constructive way, that allows room for your influence to be felt towards a profitable end for all. The freedom of their choice should be within the power of your wise discretion to direct. Being excessively possessive or yelling makes children listen less and communicate less of their fears, problem and desires to you. Mostly, when you are quick to judge, attack and do less educating the child in your actions. *It is education that sustains freedom within a profitable precinct.* The struggle in raising a child is that they are born with their own mind. *How I wish you had listened to all the good counsel given to you and discarded the bad ones, dealt with all the bad mannerism you acquire growing up.*

What is the risk of raising children under poor parenting in regards to wise nurturing?

Raising a child is one of the greatest forms of responsibility, a task that few really understand. Developing a child's spiritual, physical, social, academic and emotional need requires wisdom. Poor parenting primarily under-develop the child in all the vital areas and exposes children to many weaknesses before they become adults creating behavioural disorder. The Bible establishes this clear cut principle, *"train up a child in the way he should go: and when he is old, he will not depart from it"* **(Proverb 22:6).** What way specifically, you may ask? Good, the way of, wisdom, knowledge, understanding and the fear of God covering the other vast aspects of life. What really understanding and soothing choice? A fall is not far-fetched, struggles and instability will mark the child's experience in life.

A child can either grow into a wise person or a foolish person. *80 per cent of the crisis adults face in life stem from the lack of foundational training and wrong equipping.* However, a well-trained child can possibly end in foolish existence, and a poorly raised kid can end in the path of wisdom based on the variables that play in their lives. The reason is because, both adult and children minds are easily corrupted by the ***desires they form***; the ***information*** they are *exposed* to, the ***environment*** they live in, the ***company*** they *keep* and the ***choices*** they make. It is a known fact that good education enhances a child's thinking process, but that is not enough because children in good learning environment still miss it. *"The great aim of education is not knowledge, but action."* - **Herbert Spencer.** Until you can act what you know, your training is useless. Have you lost the good knowledge impacted on you? *Action is the proof of wisdom or the lack of it.* If life has taught you anything, it says don't be foolish! *Carefully weigh your action steps now, are they wisdom based or foolishness based?* **Wise actions yield increase and efficiency while foolish actions breed shortage and deficiency.** This is the capital difference between people and nations.

It is a hard place to be in life, living with the wrong ideas and thinking the wrong thoughts. It takes the introduction of one negative seed to have a negative tree. Ignorance does not necessarily mean foolishness; it only suggests you lack something vital, denial only confirms it. Paying attention to details will save many from sliding into a potential pitfall. When a life is governed by wisdom it will produce: good success, a good man and woman, a good home, a thriving business, good grades, quality relationships, a submissive and loyal wife, a loving and faithful man, a strategic and visionary leader, wealth and victory in life are a direct product of wisdom. Wow! I envy you right now because *a life led by wisdom always turns out right.* It is wisdom to abide in the truth and the way of truth. The truth is that man is God's object of affection, submitting to his will is the best thing you can do for yourself. The light of His word in your mind can illuminate and transform your life and direct your path. *A life without any discipline of purpose lacks judgement.* Do you condemn easily and despise people before you really get to know them? Despising your neighbour is a sign of the lack of wisdom. Harbouring bitterness and hatred towards people breaks the bound of unity needed to forge progress, why destroy the one that can potentially help you? Do you ignore good advice because you're too proud to listen and too big to be told what to do with your life? *A man operating without good counsel and good listening skill is a potential failure.* Have you let your passion led you into preventable trouble than you have use it for any productive engagement? Are you a slave to your passion? With due respect sir or ma, *when your passion becomes misleading, you are prey in the hands of an easy manipulator.*

Do you take decision without understanding the full implication?
"Action without thinking is the cause of every failure." - **Alex McKenzie.** Losing focus is losing momentum in life. A life with a focus mind or focus goal lead with advantages. What is your focus in life? Careless existence will limit your potentials dramatically. Think well before you talk, are you a careless talker? If people easily question your character and impose less confidence in you, you lack character and integrity. A bad management of money cripples your financial strength. Do you spend out of your emotion or out of cost analysis? (What will it cost me to spend this money now both on a short and long-term consideration) Never lose money carelessly again. Sit down and evaluate all the crazy and stupid things going on in your life now and cleverly address them and learn from them. Make out time to do in-search and out-search of your life today. Who do I need to avoid completely out of the way of foolishness from today onward? Change for the best. The acts of a foolish man are his worst nightmares. The multiple question laid out in this chapter is designed to help you ponder your path carefully to correct and function better.
Life is a bitter argument when foolishness traps your advantage.

CHAPTER 9

THE LAZY MIND

Laziness feeds your disadvantages and buries your dream in ruts

The lazy man or woman is a person disinclined to activity or exertion. Whenever you become indolent about your life and future you set yourself up for failure. The race of life requires energetic, competitive and vigorous individuals diligent in their pursuit of destiny with a habitual effort. When you permit idle and inactive period or mind-set in your life long enough, laziness will creep in with chains that can keep you in a bad negative cycles. Laziness left un-addressed will spawn chains of poverty and backwardness. ***Average living begins with lazy thinking***; it makes a potential champion a failure.

CAUSES OF LAZINESS

1. Procrastination 2. Inability to identify and address your weakness 3. Lack of serious commitment 4. Lack of vision 5. The loss of hope 6. Lazy friends 7. Idleness 8. Attachment to unproductive fun and social activities 9. Lack of childhood grooming and programing 10. A sense of dependency and inability to stand up for yourself 11. A faulty mind-set. 12 waiting for an inheritance or blessing mind-set 13. Lack of management skills 14. The fear of failure.

It takes one idle moment to birth another in a salient progression and order, day after day before the person is bound into a lazy mind-set and attitude that will affect his life and work. Declining from a challenging task only stripes you of the power to make good progress on time. Whenever you become very indifferent about life, with low interest and passion for work, you begin to drift gradually into a lazy mind-set that is destructive in nature. A lazy mind makes impotent decisions, trying always yet incapable of completing the task thoroughly the first time not because of external interference, but personal undoing. Lazy minds lean towards convenient and less demanding activities, party loving, hanging out longer than necessary, game lovers, doing everything but productivity. Note: *productivity is the secret of capacity building.* The only thing you build in laziness is mediocrity. People can be conditioned into a lazy state of existence when they begin to avoid high pressure task preferring to do cheap labour with their hand than really applying their mind into difficult assignment until an answer emerges.

Life has always giving you room for improvement and self-development. Pre-mature satisfaction and contentment will blind you from the next level mega improvement. (you can do better than your current level and improve on any previous achievement, get it done) if nothing propels you to achieve excellence higher than your parents, friends at all level, your community and your mentor, it is possible that you're too comfortable to make any significant change. **Laziness comfort men into a bad sleep.** *Those who sleep on the bed of laziness rise with many weaknesses.*

Who have you become or what are you becoming? Do you like who you are now? Warning; laziness will affect every aspect of your life, economically, physically, spiritually, financially and socially. Conquer it now.

Indicators that an individual is lazy;

1. A consumer lifestyle, eating but producing nothing
2. Complacency towards everything.
3. Making excuses for failing and never accepting responsibility
4. Waiting for big opportunities but never ready to find one
5. complaining about everything but lack solution for anything
6. Quit easily in the face of opposition or pressure after one or two attempts
7. Zero patience for long-term pursuit
8. Talking yourself down before people in order to avoid being tasked.
9. Zero focus for details.
10. Shallow thinking and poor depth analysis.

11. Seeking for easy escape route, permanent evasive mood.
12. Not ready to accept the challenge for freedom, the risk and the pursuit.
13. Inability to articulate your vision path for life
14. Inability to make firm decisions that matters and stay committed to it
15. Just playing along but never moving ahead

Keys to overcoming laziness: the key to triumph is to try. Develop an obsession for success and for an achievers mind-set that breaks the tradition of laziness around you.

Laziness is the mother of under development, under achievement and retrogression. To overcome laziness out of your life, you need a daily assignment to create new routine with a time frame on it. BECOME DECISIVE, QUICK AND ACTION ORIENTED. Create a daily routine that challenges your capacity to think and respond to problem creatively. Create a focus model for each week, a task and reward plan. Stop playing around with folks that can compromise your concentration. Join the company of the successful and effective time managers that will teach you priority. Create a need to achieve an uncommon excellence with a high sense of urgency. When you find yourself slip back into lazy mood jerk back to action.

Develop a do it NOW mentality, postpone noting aside until you complete it. Lazy people usually have poor esteem about themselves. Build your self-confidence and self-worth by appreciating the new improvement you make daily and stay focus on accomplishing more rewarding tasks. Substitute your easy going and fun feeling attitude for the achiever's mind-set driven by task and result. *Laziness is the ladder to the grave.* Your ability to succeed is infinite and unlimited don't stop it with laziness. **Stagnation is the burden of laziness.** The culture of lazy people is the corruption of their strength and the foundation for under achievement.

CHAPTER 10

THE FOCUS OF A CHAMPION

It takes habit to control your life outcomes; therefore, cultivating the habit of focus gives you 80 per cent control over your life.

Create a focal direction for all you do in life, which will be the centre hub of operation for you; because whatever you focus on is what you will succeed at. Success requires absolute focus on what matters without the drag of distractions and nursing the option of failure because focus must be maintained no matter how long it takes to achieve your goal. Once it is broken and discarded, progress is automatically broken. Focus creates energy to rise above the moment and energy for progress. Having a goal does not necessarily make you an instant success, because it takes a significant amount of time to pursue and achieve your goal or your dream. You will encounter difficulties and discouragement that will pose a threat on your dream sometimes. However, learning to push forward in the face of setbacks brightens your chances of making it.

Focus increases the quality of your personality as you consistently rise in results and initiates a dynamic change in your life. Men and destinies are shaped in the frame of their habitual character: life can't give you anything you are not ready to seize. Note: **life failures have controlling habits while men of success have navigation habits.** Men without focus are potential accident waiting to happen. Imagine driving without focus or direction. A cripple in the right direction beats a runner in the wrong direction. EQUATION: purpose = focus = direction = destination = success = champions.

Every careless worker or person lacks the ability to focus on the essentials. The top is designed for men of focus. 'Energy without focus is potential destroyed'. You rule your world with the focus you design for work. *Growth is the function of applied thought and the execution of focus action steps.* Therefore, time on the table of focus generate speed. Note; your world can only expand to the degree of focus applied. *A life without focus is an apology in extension; even so, speed without focus leads to possible crash.* ***"Accuracy is the measure of focus".*** Power distributed in random motion gain space without strong impact. You cannot be everywhere and achieve anything specific on time. Focus begins where purpose is redirected: a journey without an end point in mind is a trip to nowhere. Organize your thinking and you will organize your life. The man you see in your organized thought now is the life you will express eventually. ***Productive thinking is engineered by calculated focus.*** Never lose track of time, employ each minute wisely, do business that is to say value your time.

The beauty of life is hidden in the little decision we make every day. Every time you make a horrible decision you create a horrible outcome. Most times, people take decisions before they realise the impact of their choice. *A focus based action is all you need to attain any height in vision.* Whatever you do consistently in a successful fashion, will only lead to one successful conclusion. *Ask yourself what must I do today to achieve my dream?* Once you identify your action steps, it clarifies your objective and positions you with a focus drive to identify and attract the necessary opportunity and resources into your life. Those who play around without any clear objective experience little changes in life and wonder why life is difficult for them. If you don't see the treasure of focus now, you may live with trash at the end.

"Focus now and play later or play now and suffer later". The hallmark of a champion is that they prepare for the inevitable. Circumstance will challenge your dream, discouragement will set in, and you may experience opposition and distraction all in the attempt to break your focus, decide to stay one step ahead always. It is alright to retreat in the face of opposition and challenges, but it is bad news to quit because they came. Make sure your focus is right the first time because the wrong focus is misleading in nature. The right focus demands that you form the right priority, think carefully about it with useful and resourceful materials or information, and seek for good counsel that will lead you to the fulfilment of your dream.

Life can be intimidating mostly when you don't know where to begin from, confused with no clear objective, to worsen it all when your friends won't help you out and welcome you to their circle because you don't belong according to their standard. It is an awful thing to suffer rejection and inferiority complex because you will stumble on everything possible. Smile and square up for a surprise package because the 'rejected' can be celebrated. Focus on something big and achieve it and watch the world beg for your attention. *Wake up each day with the responsibility of a focused mind and step out of the shadow of yesterday's emptiness and focus all your effort on a defined goal and stay on it till it is accomplished.*

Every level of success you achieve increases your self-worth and breaks the previous existing barrier that once defines your class. For example, if your clicks once rejected you because they felt you couldn't afford a car, when you buy a better model of whatever they are driving; just at your sight, they will automatically drop their sentiments about you and seek to find how you did it. Believe me, **success is the best outcome of focus.** Watch out because the next time they organise a program you will be the first to get their invitation. *Focus plus commitment equals to dynamic progress.*

Focus is also used by animals to hunt, prey and feed on other animals for survival. I like the focus of lion predators as they usually remain motionless, targeting (sometimes hidden) and wait for prey to come within ambush distance before pouncing. Ambush predators are often camouflaged, and may be solitary animals. This mode of predation may be less risky for the predator because lying-in-wait reduces exposure to its own preys. To enjoy dynamic progress in life you should develop this focal sense to help you go for opportunities rather than wait for them. As you study further, you will see how to make the most out of the practise of focus irrespective of what you do. Do well to employ the seven key areas of focus concept expose in this chapter for you. These are tips designed to position and engage your mind in creating value and deliver profitable products to your prospects and to increase your overall performance as you seek to increase efficiency negotiation tactics and sales presentation. You can also use it to spot predators with criminal and dubious mind lurking around to attack. I distilled these wisdom keys from the animals to teach focus lessons towards good productivity.

SEVEN KEY AREAS FOR FOCUS

1. Know your target or market well, their needs, current position and reaction tendency before you approach them. 2. Develop a sense of precision in your decision analysis, pick point accuracy launch. No guess work, eyes on the prize. 3. Develop a position of advantage to lure and attract perfectly. 4. Listen intensely and observe wisely and eliminate distractions and potential threats carefully. 5. Know when to strike because timing is everything. 6. Create a perfect environment for conditioning and receptivity. Never scare a good prospect away. 7. Do not be a victim of an opposing focus web that is counterproductive.

Adaptation, (Adjust and acclimatise) **proposition** (Plan and suggest) and **strategy.** (Approach and tactics) you will need to adapt, change plans and subscribe to winning strategy to keep your focus alive. These keys are not designed to make you a prey or a predator, but to help you develop a mind-set for precise operation, yielding excellent results avoiding the pitfalls of errors, poor judgement and weak performance building mutual progress. Men and women of focus are team players with good communication skills that compliment than compete the wrong way. As a wise competitor you make your rivals follow your lead permanently. Always 10 steps ahead: get there first and seize it first through applied focus. People in sales and marketing will benefit greatly from these tips. Being committed to a life of focus will increase your life performance, productivity, and growth exponentially. *A mind designed to take focused steps win in successful fashion.*

CHAPTER 11

THE TRAP OF LIMITATIONS

*What feeds the mind will set it free. - **Bishop Noel jones.***

A man who does not know how to beat his limitations is already living in a trap. Whatever hinders the human mind to see clearly; his choice, direction, capabilities, control, resources, attraction, values, environment, hidden treasures, threats, barriers, and opportunities will limit its abilities to the boundaries of his thoughts. *The mind is only free to the degree of its strength (what it has acquired, developed and mastered) and the things it can control.* The human race as you know is full of limitations without power to life struggle will persist; in retrospect it doesn't mean that the availability of power guarantees the elimination of the traps of limitation. Note; limitation is both real and abstract in concept. (They are physical and mental limitations) there are basically created from human activities that break progress and hinder success. The world is governed by power structures both in the physical and the spiritual that help to direct and coordinate our daily activities.

Every man is born into an environment that produces some form of identical limitation attached to that place. Wherever you are in this world you must have experienced one form of obvious limitation that is peculiar to your territory. **Power in itself can produce freedom or bondage depending on who wills it.** There are primarily two forms of power, the productive life giving power and the destructive power. Power exists in units, forms and quantity. Until you have access to the right power you can't control anything willingly on your own. *Power is a construction of an idea in the imagination of its source backed with energy and force to produce certain effect.* Once you acquire control you can both limit or release any object within your grabs. The basic drive of the human nature is the pursuit of power. Why? Power produces influence and the man with power have been given ability to control people or things. For example: 1. Political control of a country or area 2. A person or an organization that has a lot of control and influence over other people or organizations. Please note; **there are inherent power and acquired power.**

All men are equipped with inherent power or ability to act or produce an effect. The brain is the seat of power that drives all of human endeavour, achievements and operations, without it you are powerless. The brain has the clout to formulate, coordinate and destroy coded into it.

Physiologically, the function of the brain is to exert centralized control over the other organs of the body. The brain acts on the rest of the body both by generating patterns of muscle activity and by driving the secretion of chemicals called hormones. *This centralized control allows rapid and coordinated responses to changes in the environment.* Some basic types of responsiveness such as reflexes can be mediated by the spinal cord or peripheral ganglia, but sophisticated *purposeful control of behaviour* based on complex sensory input requires the information integrating capabilities of a centralized brain.

It acquires information from the surrounding world, stores it, and processes it in a variety of ways. From an evolutionary-biological perspective, the function of the brain is to provide coherent control over the actions of an animal. A centralized brain allows groups of muscles to be co-activated in complex patterns; it also allows stimuli impinging on one part of the body to evoke responses in other parts, and *it can prevent different parts of the body from acting at cross-purposes to each other.*

To generate purposeful and unified action, the brain first brings information from sense organs together at a central location. It then processes this raw data to extract information about the structure of the environment. Next, *it combines the processed sensory information with information about the current needs of an animal and with memory of past circumstances.* Finally, on the basis of the results, it generates motor response patterns that are suited to maximize the welfare of the animal. These signal-processing tasks require intricate interplay between varieties of functional subsystems.

(*Source of the physiological description of the brain is Wikipedia*) let me show you more about the functions of the brain.

1. Information processing. 2. Perception. 3. Motor control. 4. Arousal. 5. Homeostasis. 6. Motivation. 7. Learning and memory as described by *Wikipedia.* I am going to present more information on 6 and 7 functions as mentioned above. According to evolutionary theory, individuals are genetically programmed to behave in ways that ensure survival and reproductive success. This over-arching goal of genetic fitness translates into a set of specific *survival-promoting behaviours*, such as seeking food, water, shelter and a mate. The motivational system in the brain monitors the current state of satisfaction of these goals and activates behaviours to meet any needs that arise.

The motivational system works largely by a reward–punishment mechanism. *When a particular behaviour is followed by favourable consequences, the reward mechanism in the brain is activated,* which induces structural changes inside the brain that cause the same behaviour to be repeated later whenever a similar situation arises. Conversely, when behaviour is followed by unfavourable consequences, the brain's punishment mechanism is activated, inducing structural changes that cause the behaviour to be suppressed when similar situations arise in the future. Almost all animals are capable of modifying their behaviour as a result of experience—even the most primitive types of worms. *Because behaviour is driven by brain activity, changes in behaviour must somehow correspond to changes inside the brain.*

Neuroscientists currently distinguish several types of learning and memory that are implemented by the brain in distinct ways:
Working memory is the ability of the brain to maintain a temporary representation of information about the task that an animal is currently engaged in. This sort of dynamic memory is thought to be mediated by the formation of cell assemblies—groups of activated neurons that maintain their activity by constantly stimulating one another.

Episodic memory is the ability to remember the details of specific events. This sort of memory can last for a lifetime. Much evidence implicates the hippocampus in playing a crucial role: people with severe damage to the hippocampus sometimes show amnesia, that is, inability to form new long-lasting episodic memories.

Semantic memory is the ability to learn facts and relationships. This sort of memory is probably stored largely in the cerebral cortex, mediated by changes in connection between cells that represent specific types of information.

Instrumental learning is the ability for rewards and punishments to modify behaviour. It is implemented by a network of brain areas centred on the basal ganglia.

Motor learning is the ability to refine patterns of body movement by practicing, or more generally by repetition. A number of brain areas are involved, including the premotor cortex, basal ganglia, and especially the cerebellum, which functions as a large memory bank for micro adjustments of the parameters of movement.

See how unique you have been designed by God with capacity beyond your current awareness carrying a head that you know little about. It will surprise you to know that with all the extensive research done on the human brain, only 10 per cent of it has been discovered. It has been said that only 10 per cent of the brain has been utilized by human being with high intelligent productive capacity of all times. This report may not include you, I'm just wondering how many percentages you might have used counting from 1-10 so far. ***The brain or the mind is the power house of all productive energy.*** Limitation exists when one unit or all units of the primary sensory organs for life coordination is tampered with such senses as vision, hearing, touch, taste and smell.

If only one unit is tampered with, you have one obvious limitation with an added advantage, but if all the units are altered, your chance of survival is reduced almost to zero where the individual will have to live on life support system. *When you have all the sensory organs working, it shapes your mind through data collections and your mind in turn shapes your world. Without the sensory organs the mind cannot imagine anything.*

Imagination is the womb of all human productivity, the engine of creative abilities and resource-fullness. *The outside world is a direct picture of imagination.* One of the greatest powers you possess is the ability to think new things. Whatever impairs your ability to think right has created a limitation for you? Yes thinking gives an individual the ability to form response, create, control, see ahead and engage wisely all of life resources placed before him. Thinking new things is the activity of imagination. Note; *if you can't imagine it, it is already impossible for you.* **Your ability to imagine and do it effectively is the key to unlocking your world. Effectiveness begins when you can imagine and do it – imagining it, is one thing, doing it or executing it - is another thing put together. If one is missing in the equation, you are limited in a significant way.**

EFFECT, VALUE AND WORK GENERATORS
Once a man loses control of his thinking, he loses control of his life and destiny. A man in control of his thinking can direct his mind towards productive activities. *You are only rich to the degree of your ability to produce effect, value and work.* The man who know how to produce **effect** search for **seeds** and **create systems, organize and govern** while the one who produces value locate *fruit* for existing market and create **distribution and supply networks.** The man that produces work increases **production capacity and efficiency and manage business operation.** Whenever a man, system or a nation lacks these three components for living a high productive life he is limited and trapped. *Are you an effect maker or value giver or a work generator?* Men and women who operate at this level of efficiency, rule, influence and control their world, where do you belong?

Political control of a country or an area: the purpose of a government is to organise society and empower her citizen through an enabling environment, create opportunity for all to attain self-actualization, eliminating all security risk to protect its own from both internal and external enemies. The battle for political control can often time create tension, war and death for the people they seek to govern. Creating an environment full of hostility that erodes economic stability and business operations. An area marked with income inequalities as a result of political controls that enrich a few set of powerful alliance in government scheme. **Conflicts and unrest**: surely will create limitations and struggles for its citizen. When a man loses his freedom of expression, right to life and its benefits: that is limitation.

Organization limitation: probably you work in an organization where you feel stocked because of office politics, conspiracy and oppression from your superiors who are bent on making it difficult for others: who you are not in terms with their style of operations, as they contravene laydown rules and protocols with impunity; thereby, placing a limitation on staffs who cannot contend with the powerful boss. It is either you leave the organization or wait patiently and work your way up. Working in an environment full of threat and intense pressure because of the kind of system you work in will only create stress and short circuit your creative energy daily. You have no obligation to stay whatsoever.

Do you have a legal limit placed on you like house arrest or a court order to stop you from achieving your plans because of a political interest or a controlling interest of powerful organization or entities? Challenges like this: exist and do require a strategy, time, money and the right men to root it. Avoid going head-to-head with a powerful structure as a quick measure approach. Attacking such formidable system without the knowledge of their strength and how far they can go to hurt you is a dangerous call.

There are areas marked with controlling group or a sect who wants to gain area dominance because of their ideology or special interest that has place a limit on men and women from conducting their daily business operation thereby posing a limitation to people's growth and you've lost hope of the situation? Please don't quit now all limitation is breakable.

I have discovered something terrible in the African setting, about its youth who have affiliation to a particular political party or an individual placed in authority; when engaged in a revealing discussion that borders on the leaders inabilities to solve a pressing generational issue plaguing the people they just enter into evasive and defensive mood immediately to cover up rather than listen and contribute objectively. Whenever people refuse to ask important questions that will address their problem squarely and stand firm with one voice until they get a lasting solution from the relevant body responsible, they pass blames and end up transferring one problem to one generation and the others because, they lack the ability to deal with the difficult question.

'Wherever people live with false ideas about their lives they permit a strong hold that forms a limitation on them.' Behind every question there is an answer, and silence or an indifferent position is also an answer. The inability of a person to provide clear and satisfying answers to life threatening questions is a major limitation. Whenever people think together they overcome together because it is the burden of leadership to solve problem. However, when leaders are divided against themselves in the face of difficulties they become the problem. Whenever it is impossible for leaders to reach reasonable agreement they put untold limitations on the people. That is limitation.

HOW TO PROVIDE RELEVANT ANSWER TO ANY PROBLEM

To be an answer provider in your generation, certain basic skills should be employed. Define the problem, then see and reason through the problem objectively without bias or favour considering its historical content and players, identify the primary source, see where the burden of the issue at hand lies, who are the victims at large, who is benefiting from it, do you have an immediate answer to it, what is the cost of delay, what do I have that is key to my answer, what do I lack, will there be casualties in an attempt to provide an effective solution and how do I protect them?

Africans are only limited to the degree or quality of the choices they make. When you have leaders and followers alike who don't want to address the difficult questions of their land, how do you expect change? Is Nigerian poor? Look around, the country has been poorly managed virtually everything entrusted to the leaders that govern it. Nigerian dilemma today is lack of accountability, the lack of wise management of our resources, lawlessness and its people. Please quote me wrong, over fifty years of independence the country has lost more money than it has saved, it has created more debt records than it has saved cash in its reserve account. The economic struggle today is not because of fall in the oil price, it is as a result of wisdom deficiency. No wonder, someone which I will not mention her name once said that ***"Nigeria is too rich to be poor, yet too poor to be rich"***

I couldn't doubt or agree more with her except you have a different view. With all the degree holders in this country and the number of intelligent minds and talents we have, yet Nigerians still doubt the fate of our own country, what an irony? Almost all the government institutions have failed the country. What a trap? ***Corruption hides in the shadow of a deceiver. Only the pleasure of deception ruins the wealth of a nation.*** What are the way forward leaders of tomorrow? *"In the end it is important to remember that we cannot become what we need to be by remaining what we are."* - **Max Depree.**

In many African countries there are instances of Gender discrimination that limit the female folks. Where girls are not allowed to go to schools, in some families and community women are not allowed to work or pursue any ambition at all. Most people cannot improve themselves and attain any form of social advancement in the absence of training, skills or education, people cannot help themselves. They cannot prevent diseases and cannot apply new ways of doing things because of the lack of Education, Training and basic skills are limited. That is limitation.

Lack of physical fitness and good health is a limitation factor like ill Health and Disability that destroy people's ability to exercise their strength in advancing their lives.

Geographic and ecological factors such as mountains, swamps, deserts and the likes have also made life condition unbearable in many places. This is why some rural areas are poorer than others, even in the same country. You also have poverty related limitations plaguing the people which are helpless on their own or can't access the required funds by any means strip of fortune and good success.

Limitations are also misconception of thoughts buried in our ignorance and poor judgement of the obvious. *The greatest victory you will have in life is addressing your limitations.* (Everybody got one) *'The point is this, whatever forms a limitation in your thinking will eventually control your possibilities'.* know yourself, define your situation and find a solution. In places like Africa and other countries where there are obvious dark spiritual powers which root is purely demonic used to harm, hunt, destroy and limit people from ever amounting to anything or make satisfactory progress? Yes it happens.

Therefore, it takes a measure of power to create any form of limitation whether spiritual or physical. Never the less, it begs for one to reason. *If you have not been trapped by the limitations of time and life, what will be your achievements?* 2. **Can I be free from my limitations in life you may ask?** Yes, by identifying the source of the one you have been trapped in and applying the required power to override it. Many have given up because they don't know how to deal with the forces that bind them.

God is the primary source of power and the distributor of the same. That is why without God in you; you are limited with physical energy alone which is frustrating, mostly when you know your needs yet can't fulfil them through any means known to you. *There are diverse forms of power in operation - only few understand its form, mode and nature. 'What you do not understand, you can't stop: not for the lack of power or the absence of it.*

It takes the knowledge of truth to satisfy the demand and supply of power. That is why Jesus said: you shall know the truth and it will make you free. It takes the power of truth to chat the course of freedom (when you know better you can do better) against all binding forces whether natural or spiritual that tends to constrict human progress.

The truth doesn't float in the air; neither is it buried in any particular culture or human tradition, even the society is devoid of it. Man cannot produce truth in and of himself because of the corruption in his desires. That is why they lie, cheat and rob.

Living without the truth is death in itself because once you are dead in ignorance you don't need a devil. Every man is crippled in the darkness and limitation of their thinking without the light of truth. *It is a natural phenomenon that light rules, controls and eliminates darkness. Hence, it takes a man in darkness to suffer the chains of limitation.*

People prefer to stay in the dark because the convenience of ignorance is less challenging than the demands of truth. Nothing gives ability like the pursuit of truth. The knowledge you acquire becomes your power against all forms of limitations.

CHAPTER 12
AVOID THE BLAME GAME
*You don't need everybody to fix your problem,
what is required is the wisdom key*

You may never live a life free of problems and disappointments, what you need are wisdom keys to deal with them when you encounter one. Every life experiences will leave a deposit in your memory book called residual effect. On the other hand, the mind tends to hold on to things it should forget and forget the things it should remember. Dwelling on the past is always counterproductive. You can't articulate progress steps successfully thinking backward on past failures all the time and make significant progress, because when the mind dwells on issues that bother it the most than issues that inspires it, you deny yourself the chance to connect with what is before you. When your mind is inspired, it draws energy from within and without that induces joy and new strength to make progress.

When your thoughts dwell on past pain, losses, who caused it, who to blame, you only recount the past experiences and walk in circles wishing it was better hurting yourself with depressive thinking. Depressive thoughts easily become torments in your body controlling your behaviour, leaning towards death tendency as your mind denies you the ability to cope with pain and respond to recovery steps. It hurts to see your dream fail, be knocked out of a promising opportunity, betrayed by a trusted friend, robbed of your innocence, mislead into a calculated trap. Here you are with a load of regrets and lost years, held bound by the choice you made or participated in. Who do you blame? Good counsel; no body! ***Life is bigger than yesterday's regrets and disappointment, invent a better tomorrow today.***

How we react and cope with the difficulties in our lives differ greatly from one person to another. Worrying can be helpful when it stimulates you to take action and solves a problem. But when the mind become preoccupied with protracted worries about the problem without any possible way out, you begin to lose strength to engage time meaningfully with your anxiety level soaring, focus broken and you allow it interrupt your daily life. Persistent anxiety and stress can lead to psychosomatic disorders, a disease that affects the mind and the body. Emotional disorder is the natural outcome of stress and deep anxiety. When we are afraid or overly anxious we may develop: a fast heart rate, personality disorder, panic disorder, a thumping heart, feeling sick (nauseated), sweating, chest pain, headaches, a knot in the stomach etc. If the people in your life have left you disappointed, emotionally broken, frustrated, financially wrecked and bitter, don't blame them forever because, by doing so, you are saying, I am not sure I can still make it, no! **Do not give your problem power over you.** It is definitely hard to move forward with dragging issues pulling you down emotionally, psychologically and physically every day of your life. *Blaming people for failing without addressing the primary cause sets you up to fail more.*

Nobody can make your life better or worse than it is now except you allow it. When you allow the negative thoughts of the past weigh you down for too long, instead of letting it inspire you, you advance into depressive mood that can impair your ability to see clearly; once your judgement is clouded you make poor choices based on feelings not facts, choices that relieve temporal pain without a permanent solution. For example some people just go into excessive drinking, taking of drugs, wasteful lifestyle – with burning thoughts like, what is good about my life, I am tired of life, no more hope for me and other vices that people permit because of pains, only to wake up with more damages to deal with. *"Never cave into a depressive lifestyle".*

A man with broken focus, broken hope, broken heart and a trapped mind is death walking among the living. Dead hearts need no burial. The bed of your thinking is the strength of your life. *Wherever your thought sleeps there your life will rise. Therefore, make the right bed.* Self-pity is the enemy of progress. You can't punish everybody in your past but you can reposition your future. Don't be punishing twice. The future is you.

How to let your condition inspire you?

1. Appreciate the situation in totality. See the beauty in it, not the heartaches and learn from your weaknesses. Whenever your mind shifts from depression to appreciation, you just stopped blaming yourself and others. It frees you from guilt and shame into solution base thinking. Note: every bad situation in life has a good solution hidden within it. Crack the code. The past left unaddressed hurt and hunt in many ways. ***Depression shows you your failures, but appreciation shows you your advantage.***
2. Define a new end for you. (do not settle for anything less than great) It is possible when you embrace a new change.
3. Birth new joy out of your pain. (the pain is there but it is no more controlling how you feel or react) If you were involved in your pain, you can be involved in your joy. Seize the chance! This joy is only dependent on what you can gain looking and moving forward.
4. Teach others your lessons and help others overcome their pains. It will reveal hidden abilities and strength in you.
5. Create or align with a new environment that allows you appreciate your progress made as against counting your losses. *One day of encouragement will propel a thousand steps forward.*
6. Gain new knowledge that can help correct the defects in you. Never consider yourself a mismatch for life whenever you are combating a particular case in your life that has kept you down on a repeated count.

A new experience awaits you if you allow yourself to believe again, to dream again and to have faith again. Things will change for the better when you accept the challenge of a new life. Two years from now you will look back on your past, over the hands that dealt with you negatively, the rough path you endured to get here and appreciate them for the input they have made in your life. *When you begin to let go, you create room for your heart to ventilate and experience healing.* Let it go? Yes, it takes time for emotional wounds to heal – find a way to let it go.

Those who let past pain propel them to make progress in life form the attitude that says, it was bad, but I got this. "I am an overcomer" they are gone for good, I have nobody to blame but me. Blame nobody and take no excuse for failure. Forgive and learn to forget it. Avoid making repeated mistakes: if you don't trust yourself to make the right decision over an issue in your life, avoid it completely, create a distance that helps you resist your demons. Study and control the emotions that make you fall cheap to it and seek for good support to help you out. If you notice that your environment doesn't inspire you anymore because of your negative association with it, do well to find one suitable for you.

Settle down to do a proper analysis and assessment of things that you must do and let go, in order to have a better life. Here are some lay down action steps for you;

1. Forgive every offender and forgive yourself for missing it
2. Learn to stand up for yourself when everybody you know has given up on you
3. Give life to whatever is dying in you (courage and strength) and around you to stay alive
4. Disconnect from any relationship that is breaking you down
5. Write down twenty things you can do to make you happy, stable, and fulfilled. Do apply yourself to it completely.

"When we correctly interpret a situation it is never as bad as we thought" – **John Gray. *If the situation was bad enough, you are good enough to turn it around for the better.*** Awaken the genius in you. Just know this; it will be wrong to assume that your entire problem will disappear in one day now that the solution is handy. You will have to overcome them daily with a goal in mind. All you must do is to

develop a fresh perspective for living: teach yourself to create new feelings, emotions the happy way, don't just labour for change, labour for peace of mind, and enjoy your pain until you meet your joy.

CHAPTER 13

BECOME AN ICON OF EXCELLENCE.

The world watches when you beat the odds, but you watch when left behind. Obstacle is records waiting to be reset- beat them. The man in front makes the rule.

The world around you is either shaping you or you are shaping it. It is either you conform to it or transform it. There are basically two types of human being, the conformers and the transformers. It is easy to conform when you give in to everything – blind obedience, trapped without a fighting power, lured easily by the charms of a seducer; conformity is born. You can't win in a crowd that makes you think like them. *Outstanding performance is not for conformists.* Transformers evolve through the huddles of life with uncommon instinct navigating the odds that tend to limit others until they beat the system. Chatting your way up towards self-fulfilment is a strong skill in human development which will determine whether you go forward or lag behind. You can't be a conformer and emerge as a shining example of light to others or as an icon of excellence.

 Making yourself a key part of shaping your world in a productive fashion that provide answers to human needs than creating one is a build up for an iconic personality. *The world doesn't owe you anything but you owe your world everything.* You give the world colour when you can shape it. It is easy to have a sense of entitlement in all we do because, that is how we were raised. My parent took part in bringing me into this world so it is their responsibility to care for me. No doubt about that, because it is only irresponsible parent that fails to raise their children well. If you are a father, a mother please don't miss the excitement of shaping your children future well. Coming from a broken home; disconnected from your parents, unloved and rejected can shape your thinking differently from a person who has had it all, well cared for and nurtured in love.

How does this disparity affect our ability to shape our world? Shaping the world is an assignment of purpose in man not a function of your background per say. Cut across the two background differences without an assignment in your life, you will be lost playing the game of time as social activities draw you. *Those who add profitable content to time are the icons of all times. It takes vision to see the ultimate out of the immediate. If you can't see anything, there is nothing to add to your world. Men are always inspired by the vision steps of others.* People learn more from emulation than instruction, therefore, step out in vision and achieve something great, worthy of emulation and be an icon of our time. If you don't judge yourself by your history, colour, background or nationality then you can carve a future step for others. What is limiting you from achieving greatness? Too afraid to try, I don't have their luck, etc. *cheap excuses make men cheap.*

You are too creative to be buried in obscurity. Life requires some level of finesse and dexterity to shine with the crown of an icon. If you help to create a criminal environment, you will only end up with pain and regrets. Those who overcome their limitations attack it with creativity, where you don't manage your life just to get along but to lead the way. Be the light for the next phase of development and civilization. Stand out with a winning edge in your family, among your pears, in your community and produce a light of reference "YOU." Do something that puts your name on the wall of time as a world changer in every good regard. Be remembered for something. **Becoming an icon of excellence is leadership.**

Who is a leader? A leader to me is a man or woman with the means, answers and knowledge for the needs and problems of others or their generation. Becoming a leader will require learning and development through a series of formal and informal education. You emerge as a leader easily when you make a critical difference and show the capacity to lead in the face of dynamic changes. People will judge you based on your performance and character. You can't lead well when you have questionable character that breeds mistrust and disloyalty. Leaders are responsible and reliable with a sense of direction, ability to guide and motivate their followers.

They are purposeful in their actions with a clear vision - ability to see function and contribute their measure of excellence to the overall success of their team or organization. They are also a bank of quick-witted ideas with relationship and people management skills. *Discipline, good manners and integrity is the hallmark of great leaders.* The strength of a leader is in his character to stay away from possible pitfalls and weaknesses that can potentially compromise his position of power. Leaders go into battles prepared to fight and win, when victory is the outcome it is expected. Nonetheless, when the opposite is true a leader has the right to be defeated but never surprised. ***"Everything rise and fall on leadership but leaders rise and fall by character".***

ATTRIBUTES FOR BECOMING A LEADER

You can move from where you are now, to a great position of power, leadership and influence by;
1. Finding your purpose for living
2. Doing what you love naturally and excel in it
3. Engage time with mastery
4. Overcome your past failures quickly
5. Discover your talent and gifting and deploy them maximally
6. Think like a leader and function like one. Be composed and organized
7. Produce value at all levels of life and increase your capacity to deliver result
8. Open the door of opportunity for others. Become an inspiration to someone
9. Build a legacy for the next generation.

Leadership role is diverse in nature from the street to community heads to the board room and to the president office. Competence is required to maintain leadership position as you build and leverage on every resource available to you to facilitate progress. Your ability to communicate effectively with your team members help to build collaborating effort in team cohesion and synergy. As a leader you a stable and profitable system.

Leaders should possess capacity to resolve conflict within team members and your organization at large. A leader ability to appoint and assign roles to members is the key to structural excellence because your organization is as weak as the weakest link in your team members. Build your team with quality training and capacity enlargement to improve their overall performance. Listen to the needs of your people and improve their welfare package to encourage and enrich them. Leadership is not about the position you occupy but the functions you perform. *"Leadership is the art of accomplishment more than the science of management"* – **General Collin Powell.**

The world faces you when you make a difference, but those who sleep on the bed of weakness don't rise early. 'Until you rise out of the shadows you can't make a difference' be the best you can be and your world will celebrate you. Iconic personality is born when people rise to the challenge of their time and conquer. Victory will always put you on the path of leadership. See your obstacles as stepping stone, not as barricades to your life success. Obstacles exist for one purpose… beat them.

CHAPTER 14
THE BEAUTY OF A QUALITY RELATIONSHIP
Everything success or failure is traceable to relationships.
Your life is as good as the relationship you build.

Relationship is the substratum for success. The worst thing you can do against yourself is to step into a bad relationship full of negativity marked with struggles, reproach, pains and regrets. ***Your life is as good as the relationship you build.*** Successful people form a habit of building and maintaining a network of high quality relationships throughout their lives; as a result, they do better, go further in life and function well in all they do. Lives sustained by quality relationship achieve great success because they enjoy decent help with fewer hindrances to the pursuit of their goal. ***Man is a product of influence and a product of self-discovery.***

The people you habitually associate with consistently will influence your behaviour, attitudes, beliefs and values. Therefore hanging around people with low expectation about themselves, zero optimism and critical about life will rub off their nature on you. Associate with people who are forward thinking, strategic movers, successful, who will push you to stand up on your feet and challenge you to see things the right way and dare the impossible? True. Why because, *association affects assimilation.*

Self-discovery is the bedrock of great achievers. When you discover your strength and potentials as against your weakness and inabilities it gives you room to develop: building on your strengths you can accomplish vastly more than the average person who haven't made any self-discovery about themselves. I once heard a story about a young lion that was raised amongst sheep, day and night he grew up to eat grass and drank water regularly with the sheep from a particular flowing river until one day they went grassing as usual and he watched a fellow lion chase after them vigorously and they will naturally flee at the sight of the lion. But after some days he stared into the water and discovered he looked exactly like the animal pursuing after them, so he decided not to run alongside with the sheep anymore. To his greatest surprise when the lion chasing after the sheep approached him instead of preying on him, he received a playful welcome as if to say, what have you been doing with those sheep? And that became a defining moment for him totally. *A Loin walking with sheep is a potential prey, while a loin walking with the likes of his kind is a potential predator.* Association shapes your outlook and conduct. Being in the right company multiplies your strength and courage. If you want to see your potential blossom, connect the right people.

Your world will revolve around the kind of relationship you keep. Therefore, find and keep relationships that will enhance your productivity, keep wise relationship and godly relationship always. "*He who walks with the wise grows wise, but a companion of fools suffer harm*" – **Proverbs 13:20.** The opposite is true. Any company that suppresses your courage and the creativity of your mind will trap your future in smallness. ***The union of limited thinkers is the convention of death***

How do I know the right friend or group for me?

1. Discover their purpose and vision path
2. Discern their tendencies by the character they display and the fundamental characteristic of that group
3. Weigh their communication impact on you
4. Watch the place they go to and the choice of their company
5. Watch their conviction and principles for living
6. Study the choice they make daily.

What kind of friend are you? Can people depend on you? Be a man and woman of unimpeachable character, an icon of excellence, say what you mean and mean what you say. Become a credible person and you will attract credible people to yourself. Moving ahead means aligning yourself with profitable people who you can be of good service to, and who can help you. *Whenever you allow yourself to make a bad choice you compromise your chance of succeeding.* It takes one significant choice to go up in the right direction or down in the wrong direction.

The beauty of a good relationship is that it shields you from falling into a bad trap of self-made errors; it can trigger the release of your potentials and force your star to shine. Mutual understanding flourishes between good partners and enhances their ability to trust each other in the face of opposition and trying moments. They fight and win together. *It is the bond of good friendship that sustains couples in marriages, where the wine of sweet romance and sparks of mutual attractions lace their union daily.* When two people commit to stay together in purpose and pursue one course of action anything is possible. *You are a living magnet in nature; you invariably attract into your life the people, situations and circumstances that are in harmony with your dominant thoughts.*

How do you deal with difficulties in relationships? Difficult people are difficult and good people live by good principles. Everybody has the potential to be good or bad in them. Without the check and balances in us beauty can become a beast in action. What do you do, when a man or a woman who is drawn into a relationship that promises beauty based on their assumptions or persuasion from their partners, but now is experiencing hell contrary to their expectations? The fact is that all relationships go through a face of difficulty and stress; a time when you are just dissatisfied without it you cannot understand your partner better. A relationship only becomes a living hell when the commitment and faithfulness used to build it is no more; eroded by the bad breathe of bitterness towards each other. Where the two parties are now moving in two opposite directions and impact Instead of producing joy and harmony of partnership, it is now generating animosity and reproach. *People only flourish in a nurturing relationship, care, love, respect, commitment, faithfulness, good sacrifice and peace of mind that under guard its success.*

The role of a man, is not just giving leadership, providing, listening, supporting, covering, coordinate, but learning to love when it is difficult: mostly when your damsel's attitude is conflicting with your expectations and you're grooming. (Acting out of character) and your ability to stay faithful in the face of lustful and misleading attraction. The role of a woman in her home is not just to build stability, a peace loving home, follow well, nurture and groom her young ones, distribute available resources effectively, understand and communicate, but learn to submit when her heart is lifted up in contention, disobedience, misleading enticement, pride, jealousy and contempt for her husband and also to stay faithful. *'In relationships whatever you abuse you destroy'.*

When a man treats his lady or wife right in the public with a web of splendour, adoring: with sweet approach and careful attention, she will respond with appreciation in the private with enduring love. Not as a due, but as a release of a fulfilled emotional need. On the other hand, when a man is appreciated, cared for, understood, celebrated in the secret, she secure a place in his heart that makes the woman or the lady his public praise. **Good experiences establishes emotional bond that is timeless in nature.** When couples value each other well there is mutual respect and undying love. When the value for your wife is high, she becomes your total attraction and jewel of peace. Same goes for the woman. *Nothing can break two couples apart that are ready to reason and communicate their happiness and frustration in a respectful and understanding way to resolve and educate each other without the interference of a third party.*

You are only compactible when you learn to listen and respond to each other responsibly without conflicts or minimal conflict. People tend to have the time to do the things that tear down their relationships, but seldom have time and the knowledge to do what is required to build their commitment. When two partners begin to abuse the rights, privileges and values of their connection, a fall is near. *Maintaining trust in a relationship is the glue for success.* A person with a tendency to confidently cheat, lying without conscience, steal and manifest other forms of negative propensities will lack the ability to build a long term quality relationship. *Relationships are sustained by quality character, knowledge and a heart to serve each other well.*

Those people which step into relationships for profit or benefits sake are easily drawn by the wind of seduction and misleading suggestions. *They will become relationship 'abusers' after the period of disguise and cover ups is over, because at this point they are careless about the impact of their actions.* A heart covered up in deception will leave you with bitter experience to share. Your ability to see it before you commit will guide you from falling. *No beautiful woman or a handsome guy can make you happy in a long run just by their attractions; only godly character crafted in good relationship skill can lead to gratifying happiness.*

Happiness shared in moments of attractions and lust is very fickle in nature easily lost in hard moments of testing truth and challenges. Trussing your future happiness to material things is the wrong sentimental attachment you can have going into a long term relationship. The availability of material goodies or luxury can only sponsor convenience, not happiness or joy. Both the rich and the poor goes through heart break in the hands of an abuser. *Are all rich people happy? No, are all the poor miserable? No. contentment begins when you are satisfied in purpose living a free life independent of any physical attachment.* The joy of any relationship is a product of understanding, commitment, service toward each other and harmony of purpose. *Nobody can sleep well on a comfortable bed with a shattered heart.* The worst thing that can happen to anybody is living in luxury, but saliently dying in misery.

Every good and faithful man can give their wives and children comfort, splendour, emotional and psychological peace and love whether they have much or less, and every good and faithful woman is contented in the ability of her husband to provide for her irrespective of the size per time. Women are the most eye-catching piece of design by God, an attraction to me from her hair to her gallant foot. Her details enchant or enrapture my mind piece by piece. In my loving arms I will give dews of precious perfume clinch to her warm embrace I desire no other. Surely she deserves heaven's perfect river of kisses, an immersion of its kind, massage with every drop of your of attention, lavish with sweet words, spoiled with good heartfelt overhauling provision and covering, wisely make her bed green with flames of passion paired in serving heat with charms of your arousal as you let her heart swim in the waters of your peaceful and everlasting cares.

Only relationships built on these principles and loving understanding grow, blossom and abide together from both side. They can inspire each other to achieve more without tearing each other down with disrespectful words. Some people seek for who is Mr Right and Mrs Right before they can marry. People are not wrong because they look different from you or whatever makes the separating factor obvious for you. They are wrong when the both parties can't agree on a common and binding principle even when they are attracted to each other.

Can two people walk together except they agree? Let me propose this thought boldly to you, the question is not whether you are Mr Right or not. *The question is, can you love the one you have chosen completely and be loved in return?* You will be amazed to see how people easily give up on each other, living with fake emotions just for temporal gains. *A union built on the wrong foundation will collapse eventually. Love must flow from two committed givers to build a lasting home.* It is not all about the right person, but loving right. *If you treat the right person in your life wrongly you lose, but if you give the right care to the wrong person the relationship suffer stress.*

Note; nobody is completely right in their thinking, understanding, behaviour and knowledge before you met them. As a matter of fact, it is always a risk to choose any body. When you say I did not know that I married the wrong person, all you are saying is, I am the wrong person for her or for him. Actually you don't need to be the right one to love the right way. *Just the right mind-set and attitude makes you a committed lover.* **Everybody is right for some body depending on the choice you make.**

A person can only become the wrong one for you when he or she deliberately oppose you, despise and hurt you intentionally. *The answer to the puzzle therefore, is know yourself before you choose and know your partner right before you allow them choose you. People do not necessarily fail in marriages because they married the wrong person; no. Failure comes when they fail to love right. Because only love corrects all wrong. Some people see the need to be loved as strange and demanding when their partners asked for more intimate time, while some do not know how to receive the gift of love lavished on them until it is lost to in-sensitivity and carelessness.*

Loving your partner means considering the pain and the joy of your partner before you act; readily available for each other. Being loved mean protecting the gift of love bestowed on you, by understanding the needs of your spouse or partner and be the hand of satisfaction and soothe-ness in his or her life. A union built on true love do not judge you by your background, tribal sentiments or language but is tied by the unity of purpose and the unity of faith serving God and each other totally.

CHAPTER 15

THE LAWS OF ABUNDANCE

We live in an abundant universe in which there is sufficient money for all who really want it and are willing to obey the laws governing its acquisition. – **Brian Tracy.**

There are governing laws for money acquisition and wealth creation. Learning the rules and living by them is all you need. The knowledge I will share with you in this chapter, will give you a new perspective about money and life. You can access or earn enough money than you have ever realised or discovered, more than you already have, invested, expanded and sustained. Two of the wisest questions you will ever ask yourself are, how does money flow in our environment and have I created enough channels of income into my life to enjoy good wealth?

Providing an accurate answer to this question will lead to financial fulfilment. *The error of an ignorant mind is that, he doesn't know he is rich or can be made rich.* Never let limited thinking stop you! A man that understands and functions in financial principles enjoys wealth. Earning money, receiving, spending, investing, multiplying, distributing and sustaining it is one the greatest form of responsibility. Mastering the art of money will lead to financial freedom. ***Never work for money because you will never get rich, instead work to multiply value generating wealth systems and you will never lack money.*** Your wealth is in the value you distribute not the amount you are paid in a job.

Money flow through:
1. Profitable and high yielding reward services
2. Quality goods or products
3. Create enriching treasures
4. Paying assets or income generating asset.
5. Addressing human needs through a business operation
6. Wealth producing ideas
7. Tradable skills
8. A network system of distribution
9. A production or manufacturing systems

It takes wisdom, understanding and skills to make money. Men of wisdom create products and services for hungry markets, while men that have the understanding of time and seasons attract riches by strategic positioning and by acquiring purchasing power. Men with high tradable skills attract favour from wealthy paying customers. Little is much in the hands of a focussed mind; therefore, money is nothing without the CAPITAL of focus. *Those who find a need and fill it sufficiently stay ahead of competitors with an organised and efficient customer service system that satisfy the demand and supply flow of their market, faster, cheaper and in a more reliable way: ready to reposition and expand into big markets make money and grow it.*
Opportunities are hidden needs – waiting to be met, unless identified. Time is always pregnant with one; unravel them. If an individual or a company can find **thirty new ways** to give her customers a new level of satisfaction more than their competitors, they will emerge as leaders of their field or industry eventually.

When a company care less about how much satisfaction customers gain from their services both short term and long term they begin to lose market share gradually. Every bad or good commendation a customer makes about your business operation will build a market perception and image for you. Create a value system that governs your life and business operation. Success is cheap when you have an increasingly satisfied individuals craving for your service or product. Make only promises that you can keep and avoid cutting corners. Integrity is the key to life promotion.

Good consistent character promotes individuals, companies and nations alike. *Because your character is a promise note, a potential money reference that can pull finances your way and a trust bond that can secure you favour or rejection.* Trust is a key element in every society today that can trigger attraction to you in a positive fashion. When trust grows in a community it produces capital flow and business opportunities to men and women based on the consistent display of character. ***Nothing last where trust is an issue, it is pivoted to success.***

because they show good ability in the face of a prospect. *No man is without an opportunity except he lacks searching power, direction, vision to make his own opportunity and passion to fight until he gets one.* Dreaming without applied work is progress denied. *Work is bringing value out of time and enriching your purpose.* You can't make a man poor whose mind is wealthy, wealth takes shape in the eyes of your understanding. Until you control income generating assets you are an economic disaster because in the wake of economic depression and recession you are not protected against the storm.

When your passive income has become more than your monthly and yearly expenses you are financially free. You can only achieve that by building an income producing asset. *Wealthy people think and live by wealth principles, while the poor think poverty and act poorly.* It is what you create out of your working hours that make you poor or rich, either by individual or team effort. *"The richest people in the world look for and build NETWORKS, everyone else look for work"* – **Robert Kiyosaki.**

Those who manage consumption lifestyle create permanent poverty. *You cannot change a poor history by creating a poor environment.* Opportunity looks for observers while wishful thinkers gaze at the difference. *'Time pays productive observers and excellent performance, while profit is sustained by value producers.'* 'Life without industry is pains'. *"The big secret of life is that there is no big secret. Whatever your goal is, you can get there if you're willing to work."* - **Oprah Winfrey.** The load of poor understanding is stress to the head. *Understanding is the crown of wealthy hands.* **"Your day is poor without a business plan".** A task driven day is the secret of achievers. Do you have a seed that can generate harvest? Plant it now! Those who plant economic seeds of wealth reap harvest of wealth. Only profitable labour generates profitable outcomes.

PATWISE 22 LAWS OF ABUNDANCE
1. Every human being is blessed with enough time to succeed when we rise to the task

3. No mind is barren of wealth making ideas, within you lies infinite innovative ideas
4. You possess natural gifting and talents
5. Every community is blessed with people and human capital; connect and sustain contact
6. Value givers are money makers
7. Eat your seed, eat your harvest. The size of your seed determines the volume of your harvest
8. There is enough money to go round, tap into the value chain
9. You can't wish your money problem to go away, become productive.
10. Think and attract abundance permanently. Thinking conditions your ability.
11. The lack of wealth generating Ideas and power to develop it, sustains poverty.
12. Money works for the wise, diligent and faithful masters
13. Poverty doesn't respect colour, age, nation or education. Just principles
14. Avoid the common mistakes people do with money
15. Create inheritance for the next generation
16. Open the gate of excellence – your mind and your world must open
17. A liberal giver tends toward plenty
18. Create a large consumer base with ever expanding potential
19. Be thankful and be a blessing
20. Walk in the covenant of the blessing
21. Never work to earn a living, work to deploy potential
22. Enjoy serving people well. Always ask what can I do for you?

REFERENCE NOTE

Bibliography

1. Mike Adenuga
2. PM Tony Blair
3. Steve Jobs
4. Bill Gate
5. Oprah Winfrey
6. Nelson Mandela
7. Henry Ford - wealthsytemlinks (powered by WordPress)

Our deepest fear is not that we are inadequate – Akeelah and the Bee (2006)
Ecclesiastic 9:11 – King James Version (KJV)

CHAPTER THREE

Professor William James of Harvard, "compared to what we ought to be, we are only half awake. We are making use of only a small part of our physical and mental resources. Stating the thing more broadly, the human individual thus lives far within his limits. He possesses powers of various sorts which he habitually fails to use."

CHAPTER FOUR

1. Michelangelo Bounarroti quote – (Goodreads, Inc)
2. It always seems impossible until it's done – Nelson Mandela
3. Everything is possible to him that believes – Mark 9:23 (NIV)
4. Believe it until you make it – Zig Ziglar
5. Knowledge is power, but only knowledge that can be applied to practical purpose in some way – Brain Tracy
6. There may be a thousand little choice in a day, all of them count – Shad Helmstetter
7. The future belongs to the competent get good, get better, be the best – Brain Tracy.

CHAPTER FIVE

If your action inspire others to dream more, learn more, do more and become more, you are leader – John Quincy Adams.

CHAPTER SIX

1. Proverb 4:23 (NIV)
2. It's not what a man knows that hurts him; it's what he knows that isn't TRUE – Josh Billings

CHAPTER SEVEN

1. There is no secret formula for learning to listen to your instincts – T. D. Jakes.
2. Others can inspire you, but ultimately the only the thing that empowers you is what lies within, and learning how to better utilize what you've been given – T. D. Jakes. (Book titled: INSTINCT)

CHAPTER EIGHT

1. Foolishness support failure – Dr Paul Enenche. (Book titled: 21 Foolish things people do)
2. Proverbs 22:15 – (NIV)
3. Proverbs 22:6 – (KJV)
4. The great aim of education is not knowledge, but action – Herbert Spencer
5. Action without thinking is the cause of every failure – Alex Mackenzie

CHAPTER ELEVEN

1. What feeds the mind will set it free – Bishop Noel Jones (Book titled: Battle for the mind)

2. Physiological function of the brain – (Wikipedia)
3. Several types of learning and memory that are implemented by the brain – (Wikipedia)
4. Nigeria is too rich to be poor, yet too poor to be rich – Condoleeza Rice.

CHAPTER TWELVE

1. When we correctly interpret a situation it is never as bad as we thought – John Gray

CHAPTER THIRTEEN

1. Leadership is the art of accomplishment more than the science of management – General Collin Powell.

CHAPTER FOURTEEN

1. Proverbs 13;20 (NIV)

CHAPTER FIFTEEN

1. We live in an abundant universe in which there is sufficient money for all who really want it and are willing to obey the laws governing its governing its acquisitions – Brain Tracy
2. The richest people in the world look for and build networks, everyone else looks for work – Robert Kiyasoki (Book titled: the 21st century business)
3. The big secret of life is that there is no big secret. Whatever your goal is, you can get there if you're willing to work – Oprah Winfery.

www.ingramcontent.com/pod-product-compliance
Lightning Source LLC
Chambersburg PA
CBHW050010230526
45465CB00003BB/1352